D0811867

LEAVING ANOTHER KINGDOM

SELECTED POEMS

Gerald Stern

PERENNIAL LIBRARY

HARPER & ROW, PUBLISHERS, New York
Grand Rapids, Philadelphia, St. Louis, San Francisco
London, Singapore, Sydney, Tokyo, Toronto

FIRST EDITION

Designed by Alma Orenstein

Library of Congress Cataloging-in-Publication Data

Stern, Gerald, 1925–
    Leaving another kingdom : selected poems / Gerald Stern.
        p.   cm.
    Includes index.
    ISBN 0-06-055187-9
    ISBN 0-06-096455-3 (pbk.)
    I. Title.
    PS3569.T3888A6   1990
    811'.54—dc20   89-45721

90 91 92 93 94 MV/RRD 10 9 8 7 6 5 4 3 2 1

90 91 92 93 94 MV/RRD 10 9 8 7 6 5 4 3 2 1 (pbk.)

For Ida, Patricia, Rachael and David Stern

Contents

I | REJOICINGS (1973)

II | LUCKY LIFE (1977)

III | THE RED COAL (1981)

IV | PARADISE POEMS (1984)

V | LOVESICK (1987)

I REJOICINGS

1973

THE BITE

I didn't start taking myself seriously as a poet
until the white began to appear in my cheek.
All before was amusement and affection—
now, like a hare, like a hare, like a hare,
I watch the turtle lift one horrible leg
over the last remaining stile and head
for home, practically roaring with virtue.
    Everything, suddenly everything is up there in the mind,
    all the beauty of the race gone
    and my life merely an allegory.

REJOICINGS

I put the sun behind the Marlborough Blenheim
so I can see the walkers settling down
to their long evening of relaxation
over the slimy piers.

I put the clouds in their place and start the ocean
on its daily journey up the sand;
I reach the beach a minute after the guards
have chased the last sleepers from their blankets.

Haley's blimp
drags its long tail across the sky
as the light from Greenland dips down
for a quick look at my broken stick.

I make a good circle before digging
so I can close the whole world in my grip
and draw my poor crumbling man
so that his tears fall within the line.

The sand, half out of focus, lightens and darkens
according to the clouds and the sun
and takes all I have of pity and fear
like a weak and devoted friend.

A few black puffs, the end of some great violence,
blow into the wind before their dispersal.
I move my lips and raise my quiet hand
in all the craziness of transferred emotion.

After twenty years of dull loyalty
I have come back one more time to the shore,
like an old prisoner—like a believer—
to squeeze the last poetry out of the rubbish.

I pour a little mud on my head
for the purification
and rub the dirty sand into my shirt
to mix everything with crystal.

I put a piece of shell for killing birds
in the open hand
and all the paraphernalia of the just,
bottle and paper and pencil,

for the work to come.
I wait one hour. That is the time it takes
to free the soul, the time it takes
for reverence.

Once or twice I have to alter the grave
so the water can come in quietly.
I am burying our Nietzsche;
I am touching his small body for the last time.

THIS IS LORD HERBERT MOANING

This is Lord Herbert moaning and sighing over his lost manuscripts.
This is meek old Blake wandering down the street with his wolf's
    face on.
Lamb, Lamb is a master—Marvell, Sidney, beautiful, beautiful.
A whole world of lucid and suffering poets talking to themselves.
I dream almost steadily now of interpenetration,
but not with beasts—I have had that for twenty years—
I begin with sanity now, I always begin with sanity.
—After a period of time the old lobster crawls back into his cave;
after a period of time the wise Indian puts on female clothes.
I watch them with love;
my own poor ghost would like to smash everything,
woods and all, cave and all;
I have to smother him with kisses,
I have to carry him from the room,
I have to show him what darkness is, what brightness is.
For twenty years, without knowing the name, I fought against beasts,
but my whole life is centered now in my lips
and their irruptions.
    It is beautiful watching the sun slip through the bent fingers.
    It is beautiful letting the brain move in and out of its own
        cloudbank.

IN KOVALCHIK'S GARDEN

It is dusk, the drive-ins are opening, the balloon is coming to rest.
Out of the east, so fitting, the cardinal moves into the light.
It is the female, almost too small and shabby for its splendor.
Her crest opens out—I watch it blaze up.
She is exploring the dead pear tree.
She moves quickly in and out of the dry branches.
Her cry is part wistful, part mordant.
She is getting rid of corpses.

THE BLESSED

He who destroys, he who reigns, he who meditates;
now, more than ever before, these are the three.
It is life simplifying itself,
the head cut off and the face lifted.
It is the brown rabbit dying of its fever;
it is the gray one surviving.
It is the little house of justice.
It is the dead picking flowers, dancing and eating corn.
It is the new one waving his sheaf.
It is the old one wiping his eye.
It is the Eagle Knight shaking the whole desert with his passion.
It is the strange pity of Rimbaud.
It is the strange pity of Browning. It is the towers meeting.
It is the soul of Whitehead moving into its last obscurity.
It is Walter Savage Landor's dream of entablature.
It is Walter Savage Landor in the eighteenth century.
It is Landor's hatred of kings. It is Landor's mind.
It is Landor's ceremony. It is Landor's violence.
It is the life. It is the vile reduction.
It is the new one picking flowers.
It is the old one wiping his nose, waving his eye.
It is the terror of criticism.
It is the torment of money.
It is the weariness of work.
It is the gravity of love. It is the dignity of isolation.

THE NAMING OF BEASTS

You were wrong about the blood.
It is the meat-eating lamb we are really terrified of,
not the meat-eating lion.
The noisy Soul shrieking and spitting and bleeding set us off—
the smell of nice clean grass confused us.
It is the eyes, it is the old sweet eyes showing just a little fear.
It is the simple mouth full of honest juices.
It is the little legs crossed at the bony joints.
—It is not greed—it can't be greed—it is fasting;
it is not divorce—it is custody;
it is not blood—it is supineness.

THE UNITY

How strange it is to walk alone,
the one leg never growing tired of the other;

the ears still beautiful but the sound
falling in new places;

all that I formerly believed in
explained and sweetened.

I have to concoct my own past now
out of old inhalations.

I have to live in two lives
with the same blood.

I have to separate the thirsts
without hatred.

It is a good desert—
snakes and horses—

cooks, whores, doctors—
ghosts, vistas,

women and men of all sizes and all ages
living together, without satire.

HIS ANIMAL IS FINALLY A KIND OF APE

His animal is finally a kind of ape—after all—and not an elephant,
a release for him, but more than that for the two exhausted beasts.
For years he struggled between them
and it was either the violence of the one or the obscurity of the other,
either way, as it seemed to him then, a concealment,
but now that the choice was made
they could move back into a simple relationship with him, and with
     each other.

What is amazing is the choice itself.
You would expect him to move from elephants into owls
or into the seal-like creatures or into pelicans,
or at least—if he had to go back—back now into hares—
or shrews and weasels, if what he needed was viciousness.
At least you would never expect him to choose the ape again,
not after three hundred years of greed and malice,
but what he was after was not the choosing of new animals
but another collaboration with the old ones,
and for this purpose the ape now more than the elephant
would suit his fever, or what there was left of it.

I remember sitting and talking for hours about the elephant.
I remember the room trembling with belief
and I hesitate, out of loyalty, to do any harm to that beast.
But it is he who will be free at last of *my* compulsion,
and able to graze, and able to panic,
without my interference.
The ape is different—it will be years before he is free:
in the meantime, when we rise we will rise for each other
and when we howl it will be in each other's faces.

There is nothing degrading or cynical in this.
We had to go back again for the sake of all three.
Otherwise we would mix our disgust forever with our dream.
What the ape does is separate once and for all the one from the other.
What he does is illuminate the distance.
What he does is make it bearable.
The leaves sticking out of his mouth, the puffed-out belly, the dirt on
     his lips,
this I pity;

the muzzled face, the musk-like odor,
this I pity.
I lived and I lived constantly on the verge of a true destruction.
Because of these animals I was able to break away.
I am in their debt.

ON THE FAR EDGE OF KILMER

I am sitting again on the steps of the burned out barrack.
I come here, like Proust or Adam Kadmon, every night to watch the
    sun leave.
I like the broken cinder blocks and the bicycle tires.
I like the exposed fuse system.
I like the color the char takes in the clear light.
I climb over everything and stop before every grotesque relic.
I walk through the tar paper and glass.
I lean against the lilacs.
In my left hand is a bottle of Tango.
In my right hand are the old weeds and power lines.
I am watching the glory go down.
I am taking the thing seriously.
I am standing between the wall and the white sky.
I am holding open the burnt door.

THE POEM OF LIFE

Why should our nation, into whose purses of charity are poured countless dollars, permit the birds of her land, her poets, to suffer scorn and privation?

ROBERT SUMMERS, *My Poem of Life*

For three days now I have been watching the blue jay take over—
my soul there, shrieking and squalling,
nodding and jerking its head, fluting its tail.
All day Friday it moved nervously between the two maples.
All day Saturday it hopped through the garbage collecting wisdom.
Today it is Sunday, June 4, 1968—I have *marked* it.
My wife and Bob Summers' wife and the little stoned dancer
have driven to New York to look at Martha Graham's old age.
Summers and I are sitting under the honeysuckles
smoking parodis and discussing the poem of life.
Once he had it down to thirteen words—
the Napoleonics, the logic, the letters of pride,
the six demonstrations, the five assumptions,
all his anger and irony, all his honesty,
his dream of the theater, his terror, his acts of power—
reduced to thirteen words.
—The blue jay is youth, right?—
clawing his chin, stuffing his belly, fighting the dove, fighting the owl,
filling the lawns and woods with his violent sounds.

By eight o'clock everything will be quiet here.
The miserable family upstairs will slam their back door,
the jays will disappear into the maples
and we will have the yard to ourselves.
We will go on for hours,
moving our lips, waving our parodis,
seizing and judging everything that comes
into the range of our brutal memories,
two delectable Jews,
spending our happy and cunning lives
in the honeysuckles.

THE SUPREME SUBJECT

Pittsburgh, 1967

At an unexpected turn in the Kiskiminetas
I suddenly saw again what the valley looked like
before the Scotchman came with his bitter stick.
—It is what we spent our youth arguing over:
the beauty of the rivers before the settlement
and the horror after.
The supreme subject! Contracted in our lives!
    We talked through smoke—in Hell—like fiery puddlers,
rubbing the cinders out of our hair and spitting
out clinkers.
    It was sad, really—
we couldn't even enjoy the dreams of the Tortured,
our Hell was so literal.
Not that we were advanced. God! God!
We were just getting into the sensitive
when everyone else was moving on to the vile,
and when we looked up
our eyes were red with poverty as well as grime.

Gilbert went to Provence; I went to Batsto;
and Hazley went to the mountain.
But what I write about—
and I think what we all write about—
is someway connected with the memory of that darkness
and our escape.

For the rest, I have no heart:
Thomas Mellon howling among the Presbyters.
Frick bleeding.
Berkman raging.
The reconciliation. The conversion.

    Entelechy? The Soul?

Well, we do have interesting place names in western Pennsylvania.
Everybody knows Blueball and Intercourse down there in the East,
but we have irony, our cities are named after trees,
trees and animals, and of course millionaires, and of course Indians.
—Kiss, kiss Mamma for me. Say hello to your Mary.
Goombye, Hunkies. Goombye, goombye, Hunkies.

13

WHEN I HAVE REACHED THE POINT OF SUFFOCATION

When I have reached the point of suffocation,
then I go back to the railroad ties

and the mound of refuse.
Then I can have sorrow and repentance,

I can relax in the broken glass
and the old pile of chair legs;

I am brought back to my senses
and soothed a little.

It is really the only place I can go
for relief.

The streets, the houses, the institutions,
and the voices that occupy them,

are too hard and ugly
for any happiness

and the big woods outside
too full of its own death—

I go to the stone wall,
and the dirty ashes,

and the old shoes,
and the daisies.

It takes years to learn how to look at the destruction
of beautiful things;

to learn how to leave the place
of oppression;

and how to make your own regeneration
out of nothing.

LOST WITH LIEUTENANT PIKE

How was I to know—in 1938—that anyone but
Zebulon Pike could be the master of my imagination

or that the one book belonging to my dead sister—*Alice in
Wonderland*—did not have to lie for twenty years, hidden
on a closet shelf

or that I was allowed to throw out my stupid molds, my
set, that never once, with all my pouring, managed to make
one soldier without a leg missing or without an incredible
wound in the side of his neck.

Slowly I became a man, and as I did I looked back with
shame, which was the lawful payment for my ignorance and
        meekness.

Whatever I have to do now to outlive my string of errors I will do,
and I will live as divided as I have to, and as loose and as senseless.

In another life it will be all masted vessels and sugar houses
and tea-pouring and little men running down their lanes;
this time around there will be no government for anyone.

I have to live on the lid of Hell, poor friend;
I have to leave the woods and the Shul and the chicken
standing on its wings and the white silk scarf
and the visit from Mars and the long journey to Harrisburg, Pa.

It is something to stand on a hill in the middle of November,
9,000 miles from Jerusalem, with the ice forming
inside your nostrils, and to feel your own wisdom.

IMMANUEL KANT AND THE HOPI

There was a time
when the only friends I had were trees
and the only pleasure I had
was with my crippled soldiers and my glue.
I don't say this aloud
out of any sickening desire to bring back the sensitive years,
like little Lord Christ
over in the Blue House,
but only because I am spending more and more of my time
        remembering
as my eyes change.
I guess you should weep for me because I am thinking,
like the silk merchants of Easton in their meditation rooms,
and the dead barbers in their chairs,
and the gorillas on their stone seats.
I could spend about ten good years
bringing the things together
that go into my brain,
ten good years on the river
watching the spars and the starved deer and the bathtubs float by.
    Up the street McCormick lies in wait for me,
hoping to help me with my tires and my trees
and down the street Repsher senior burns and burns,
an abused man, living on anger.
I go in and out of this road every day now
as you do on an island.

My house, with its nine white pillars,
sits peacefully on the ground
and I am the strange man
who has moved into the ruin.
From now on I am going to have something to think about
when I drive into the parking lots;
I am going to be refreshed when I walk over the asphalt;
I am going to live on two levels, like a weasel.

It is spring; 1971.
I am looking through my open windows at the Delaware River.
I am looking through the locust trees that grow here like weeds.

This summer I am going to strip some of the delicate leaves from their
     stems;
I am going to swim over to Carpentersville;
I am going to write twenty poems about my ruined country.
     Please forgive me, my old friends!
I am walking in the direction of the Hopi!
I am walking in the direction of Immanuel Kant!
I am learning to save my thoughts—like
one of the Dravidians—so that nothing will
be lost, nothing I tramp upon, nothing I
chew, nothing I remember.

IN CARPENTER'S WOODS

This is a corner of heaven here,
the moss growing under the leaves,
the rocks cropping up like small graves under the trees,
the old giants rotting in the shade.
I used to come here every Sunday
to stand on the bridge and look at the bird-watchers.
Once I made love in the dead brush
and slept impaled on the thorns, too tired to move;
once I gave myself up to the *New York Times*
and buried myself in sections a whole afternoon;
once I played football with the radicals
while the sun and the rain fought for control.
      At the bottom of the hill where the trees give way to grass
a creek runs through a silent picnic ground
almost a mile away from any access.
Here the neighborhood dogs broke into their runs
at the first threat of authority.
Here the exhibitionists came out in the open
after the long morning with the squirrels and flickers.
Here the Jehovah's Witnesses lay down their arms
and gathered quietly around the tables.
—Without knowing the name or the reason
I gave myself up to vertigo;
I lay for hours with my eyes closed listening to the great sounds
coming in from Germantown;
I loved the ground so much that I had to hold on to the grass for bal-
      ance.
   I can tell you that where those two girls go carefully over the
      stones,
and where that civilized man and his son
pick up loose wood for the fireplace
was, for three years, my refuge.
I can tell you that I have spent half a lifetime hunting for relief,
that in the simplest locations, in libraries,
in drug stores, in bus stations—
as well as under stone bridges and on hillsides—
I have found places to wait and think.

I tell you that world is as large as the one you sigh and tremble
        over;
that it is also invulnerable and intricate and pleasurable;
that it has a serious history;
that it was always there, from the beginning.

TURNING INTO A POND

All I need is one foot in the mud
to keep my sanity.
That way the water snakes can swim through my blood
and the greedy pickerel can hide
under my leaves.
All I have to do is fall asleep in the water
and let the yellow lights turn from gold to brown
as I sink to the bottom.
When it rains I can lie face down in the lilies
and let the naked couples rest their tired legs on my back.
When it gets dark I can sing to them about insanity
and compare my community to theirs.
I will release information softly,
using a deep voice for emphasis,
telling them one thing at a time.
At night I will slow down
and drift with the zooplankton.
I will dream about Voltaire and his white feet,
about Mozart and his hands.
The large mammals will waddle down to the shore
and drop their heads into the water.
The dragonfly will pull in its murderous lip
and the fisher spider will rest on its line.
In a century or two the beavers will turn me into a meadow
and my muddy wife will walk over my chest listening for cattails.
We will be so far apart it will take us weeks to reach each other.
Going by road you will be able to point me out when you get to Two
    Bridges,
in back of Penn Run, in Indiana County.
The weeds and grasses are beginning to struggle for attention;
the water is turning warm; we are going into April.

II | LUCKY LIFE

1977

BEHAVING LIKE A JEW

When I got there the dead opossum looked like
an enormous baby sleeping on the road.
It took me only a few seconds—just
seeing him there—with the hole in his back
and the wind blowing through his hair
to get back again into my animal sorrow.
I am sick of the country, the bloodstained
bumpers, the stiff hairs sticking out of the grilles,
the slimy highways, the heavy birds
refusing to move;
I am sick of the spirit of Lindbergh over everything,
that joy in death, that philosophical
understanding of carnage, that
concentration on the species.
—I am going to be unappeased at the opossum's death.
I am going to behave like a Jew
and touch his face, and stare into his eyes,
and pull him off the road.
I am not going to stand in a wet ditch
with the Toyotas and the Chevies passing over me
at sixty miles an hour
and praise the beauty and the balance
and lose myself in the immortal lifestream
when my hands are still a little shaky
from his stiffness and his bulk
and my eyes are still weak and misty
from his round belly and his curved fingers
and his black whiskers and his little dancing feet.

THE POWER OF MAPLES

If you want to live in the country you have to understand the power
    of maples.
You have to see them sink their teeth into the roots of the old locusts.
You have to see them force the sycamores to gasp for air.
You have to see them move their thick hairs into the cellar.
   And when you cut your great green shad pole
you have to be ready for it to start sprouting in your hands;
you have to stick it in the ground like a piece of willow;
you have to plant your table under its leaves and begin eating.

AT BICKFORD'S

You should understand that I use my body now for everything
whereas formerly I kept it away from higher regions.
My clothes are in a stack over against the orange pine cupboard
and my hair is lying in little piles on the kitchen floor.
I am finally ready for the happiness I spent my youth arguing and
    fighting against.
    Twenty years ago—walking on Broadway—
I crashed into Shaddai and his eagles.
My great specialty was darkness then
and radiant sexual energy.
Now when light drips on me I walk around without tears.
—Before long I am going to live again on four dollars a day
in the little blocks between 96th and 116th.
I am going to follow the thin line of obedience
between George's Restaurant and Salter's Books.
There is just so much feeling left in me for my old ghost
and I will spend it all in one last outburst of charity.
I will give him money; I will listen to his poems;
I will pity his marriage.
—After that I will drift off again to Bickford's
and spend my life in the cracked cups and the corn muffins.
I will lose half my hatred
at the round tables
and let any beliefs that want to overtake me.
On lucky afternoons the sun will break through the thick glass
and rest like a hand on my forehead.
I will sit and read in my chair;
I will wave from my window.

STRAUS PARK

If you know about the Babylonian Jews
coming back to their stone houses in Jerusalem,
and if you know how Ben Franklin fretted
after the fire on Arch Street,
and if you yourself go crazy when you walk through
     the old shell
on Stout's Valley Road,
then you must know how I felt when I saw Stanley's Cafeteria
boarded up and the sale sign out;
and if you yourself mourned when you saw the back wall settling
and the first floor gone and the stairway gutted
then you must know how I felt when I saw the iron fence
and the scaffold and the plastic sheets in the windows.
—Don't go to California yet!
Come with me to Stanley's and spend your life
weeping in the small park on 106th Street.
Stay with me all night! I will give you
breast of lamb with the fat dripping over the edges;
I will give you the prophet of Baal
making the blood come.
Don't go to California with its big rotting sun
and its oleanders;
I will give you Sappho
preparing herself for the wind;
I will give you Mussolini
sleeping in his chair;
I will give you Voltaire
walking in the snow.
—This is the dark green bench
where I read Yeats,
and that is the fountain where the Deuteronomist sat
with his eyes on the nymph's stomach.
I want you to come here one more time
before you go to California;
I want you to see the Hotel Regent again
and the Edison Theater
and the Cleopatra Fruit Market.
Take the iron fence with you

when you go into the desert.
Take Voltaire and the Deuteronomist
and the luscious nymph.
Do not burn again for nothing.
Do not cry out again in clumsiness and shame.

ON THE ISLAND

After cheating each other for eighteen years
this husband and this wife are trying to do something with the three
days they still have left before they go back to the city;
and after cheating the world for fifty years these two old men
touch the rosy skin under their white hair and try to remember
the days of solid brass and real wood
before the Jews came onto the island.
They are worried about the trees in India
and the corruption in the Boy Scouts
and the climbing interest rate,
but most of all they spend their time remembering
the beach the way it was in the early thirties
when all the big hotels here were shaped like Greek churches.

Me, I think about salt
and how my life will one day be clean and simple
if only I can reduce it all to salt,
how I will no longer lie down like a tired dog,
whispering and sighing before I go to sleep,
how I will be able to talk to someone
without going from pure joy to silence
and touch someone
without going from truth to concealment.

Salt is the only thing that lasts on this island.
It gets into the hair, into the eyes, into the clothes,
into the wood, into the metal.
Everything is going to disappear here but the salt.
The flags will go, the piers,
the gift shops, the golf courses, the clam bars,
and the telephone poles and the rows of houses and the string of cars.

I like to think of myself turned to salt
and all that I love turned to salt;
I like to think of coating whatever is left
with my own tongue and fingers.
I like to think of floating again in my first home,
still remembering the warm rock
and its slow destruction,
still remembering the first conversion to blood
and the forcing of the sea into those cramped vessels.

BURYING AN ANIMAL ON THE WAY
TO NEW YORK

Don't flinch when you come across a dead animal lying on the road;
you are being shown the secret of life.
Drive slowly over the brown flesh;
you are helping to bury it.
If you are the last mourner there will be no caress
at all from the crushed limbs
and you will have to slide over the dark spot imagining
the first suffering all by yourself.
Shreds of spirit and little ghost fragments will be spread out
for two miles above the white highway.
Slow down with your radio off and your window open
to hear the twittering as you go by.

THE SENSITIVE KNIFE

Every day the dark blue sky of brother Van Gogh
gets closer and closer,
and every day the blue gentians of brother Lawrence
darken my eyes.
It is blue wherever I go,
walking the towpath,
climbing the stone island,
swimming the river,
and everywhere I sit or kneel
the blue goes through me like a sensitive knife.

I am following my own conception now
and during the night I flap my two-foot wings
in the black locusts.
I move thoughtfully from branch to branch,
always loving the stiffness and shyness
of the old giants.
I think of my own legs as breaking off
or my wings coming loose in the wind
or my blossoms dropping onto the ground.

Across the river the sticks are coming to life
and Mithras and Moses and Jesus are swaying and bowing
in all directions.
I swim carefully through the blood
and land on my feet on the side of Carpenter's Hill.
There on a flat rock
my father is placing the shank bone
and the roasted egg on a white napkin.
I climb over the rhododendrons and the dead trees to meet him.

THE ONE THING IN LIFE

Wherever I go now I lie down on my own bed of straw
and bury my face in my own pillow.
I can stop in any city I want to
and pull the stiff blanket up to my chin.
It's easy now, walking up a flight of carpeted stairs
and down a hall past the painted fire doors.
It's easy bumping my knees on a rickety table
and bending down to a tiny sink.
There is a sweetness buried in my mind;
there is water with a small cave behind it;
there's a mouth speaking Greek.
It is what I keep to myself; what I return to;
the one thing that no one else wanted.

LET ME PLEASE LOOK INTO MY WINDOW

Let me please look into my window on 103rd Street one more time—
without crying, without tearing the satin, without touching
the white face, without straightening the tie or crumpling the flower.

Let me walk up Broadway past Zak's, past the Melody Fruit Store,
past Stein's Eyes, past the New Moon Inn, past the Olympia.

Let me leave quietly by gate 29
and fall asleep as we pull away from the ramp
into the tunnel.

Let me wake up happy, let me know where I am, let me lie still,
as we turn left, as we cross the water, as we leave the light.

ON MY POOR ROAD

On my poor road there is nothing but opossum and groundhog,
the two vegetables of the animal kingdom;
no skunk, no deer, no beaver—not even a small snake
to ruin the balance;
only easy digging, and soft chewing, and staring at the sky.

On my poor road a man lives like a slug;
he rides along the soil like an old wheel,
leaving a trail of silver,
and makes his home in the wet grass and the flowers.
He is finally free of all the other mysteries
he had accepted
and sees himself suddenly lying there warm and happy.

At night he drinks his water by the dark stove
while the small radio moans
and the heart breaks in two to the words of old songs
and the memory of other small radios in other gardens.

BLUE SKIES, WHITE BREASTS, GREEN TREES

What I took to be a man in a white beard
turned out to be a woman in a silk babushka
weeping in the front seat of her car;
and what I took to be a seven-branched candelabrum
with the wax dripping over the edges
turned out to be a horse's skull
with its teeth sticking out of the sockets.
It was my brain fooling me,
sending me false images,
turning crows into leaves
and corpses into bottles,
and it was my brain that betrayed me completely,
sending me entirely uncoded material,
for what I thought was a soggy newspaper
turned out to be the first Book of Concealment, written in English,
and what I thought was a grasshopper on the windshield
turned out to be the Faithful Shepherd chewing blood,
and what I thought was, finally, the real hand of God
turned out to be only a guy wire and a
pair of broken sunglasses.
I used to believe the brain did its work
through faithful charges and I lived in sweet surroundings for the
      brain.
I thought it needed blue skies, white breasts, green trees,
to excite and absorb it,
and I wandered through the golf courses dreaming of pleasure
and struggled through the pool dreaming of happiness.
Now if I close my eyes I can see the uncontrolled waves
closing and opening of their own accord
and I can see the pins sticking out in unbelievable places,
and I can see the two lobes floating like two old barrels on the Hud-
      son.
I am ready to reverse everything now
for the sake of the brain.
I am ready to take the woman with the white scarf
in my arms and stop her moaning,
and I am ready to light the horse's teeth,
and I am ready to stroke the dry leaves.
For it was kisses, and only kisses,
and not a stone knife in the neck that ruined me,

and it was my right arm, full of power and judgment,
and not my left arm twisted backwards to express vagrancy,
and it was the separation that *I* made,
and not the rain on the window
or the pubic hairs sticking out of my mouth,
and it was not really New York falling into the sea,
and it was not Nietzsche choking on an ice cream cone,
and it was not the president lying dead again on the floor,
and it was not the sand covering me up to my chin,
and it was not my thick arms ripping apart an old floor,
and it was not my charm, breaking up an entire room.
It was my delicacy, my stupid delicacy,
and my sorrow.
It was my ghost, my old exhausted ghost,
that I dressed in white, and sent across the river,
weeping and weeping and weeping
inside his torn sheet.

MENTIONING OF THE SOULS

If I get up one more time in the dark
you will have to cover me up completely
I will be shaking so much from the cold.
And if my voice trembles as I go from room to room
you will have to leave your own luxury
to see if I am just moaning or already talking to the dead.
If you come into the kitchen
you will see how painful it is
to cross over to the dark stove;
if you sit with me one whole night
you will see how slow the hours go
in front of the hanging plants.
Stand by the crowded window for five minutes
and watch the light come in through the crippled birch.
You can laugh a little
at my wolfish soul staring at the moon;
you can close your eyes
as I say the names,
and remember, with your own lips,
as I go over the victories and the failures.

SELF-PORTRAIT

When I turn the ceiling light on
the sky turns purple and the bathroom window is filled
with a mountain of crooked limbs like a huge Van Gogh.
When I turn it off the details change,
the trunks appear, the ducks walk up the grass
and the candles begin to shine in the dark canal.
In either case I am looking at two large gum trees
sweetly shaped by years of care and now
left alone to live or die slowly and peacefully.
I will think about them all day and dream about staying here
like a secret body at the window while they change in the light
from snarled twig to violent branch to limb with shadow;
and I will dream about standing out there on the towpath
staring back at myself in this large empty house.
        Others will go to Paris, sit at the tables,
and do the River, and do the Boulevard;
I will stand at the window dressed like a prisoner
in old corduroys and Brown's Beach vest and jacket
fingering the stamped buttons and testing the pockets.
I will look at my greenish eyes in the mirror
and touch my graying hair and twist my hat.
I will think of Van Gogh in Brussels raging
against the bourgeois world, I will think of him
working all day in the sun, I'll think of him in shock;
and I will think of myself sitting in Raubsville,
the only Jew on the river, counting my poems
and—finally—counting my years; and I will think of
Van Gogh when he headed south, I will think of him giving his
life to the art of the future, I will think of his poverty,
I will think of his depressions and exaltations;
I will think of him with yellow straw hat and pipe;
I will think of him with fur cap and bandaged ear;
I will think of him against the whirling lines,
small and powerful in the hands of the blue God;
and I will think of myself walking down my road
between the rows of dogs—so familiar now
that only one still barks, the horrible Schoene,
clawing her concrete and biting her twisted fence,
and I will think of my weeds and watery places
where I can go to rest between the scourges,
and I will think of New York just two hours away

still rotting and gleaming in the golden dust.
—I will think of myself in my rabbi's suit
walking across the marshland to my car;
I will think of myself in black beard and corncob
dragging the hay or leaning against a locust;
and I will think of the mad existence of all artists
as they lean against trees, and doors, and I will look with
horror at the vile ones, the bugs eating up our leaves,
and I will dream of another artistic life for
the fiftieth time, of a small decayed city
half buried in sand, surrounded by trees and water,
with artists living together, with old newspapers lying
piled up under the porches, with that whole race
of mothers and carpenters and gardeners
living inside their houses and in their yards.
   For the sake of Van Gogh I will dream it, for the sake of his
        olive trees,
for the sake of his empty chair, for the sake of his Bible,
for the sake of his inflamed eyes, for the sake of his wild mind;
and for the sake of his black Belgians retching and gasping for air
and for the sake of his Londoners stumbling over the greasy cobbles
and for the sake of his exhausted farmers stabbing at their potatoes
and for the sake of all the lunatics of God, for the sake of the flesh-
eaters gathering after work at the Authority, for the sake of
the wagons and baby carriages lined up outside the Armory, for the
        sake of
the frozen Armenians going back into their empty towns, for the
        sake of
the Jews of Vilna waiting inside their synagogues and for the sake of
the naked boys moving between the numbered tables and for the sake
of the slowly moving bodies under Lexington Avenue and for
the sake of the horses that labored quietly for three thousand
years and for the sake of the unassimilated wolves who lay trapped
inside their own forests; and in memory of the first stones we dragged
out of the mountain and in memory of the Fire
out of which the burned doves flew looking for water
and in memory of the long life that stretches back now
almost a million years and in memory of the cold rain
that saved our lives and in memory of the leaves
that helped us breathe and in pleasant memory
of the grass that clung to our slippery arms and legs
and in memory of the nourishing sand in which we lay like dead
        fishes
slowly mastering the sky. In honor of Albert Einstein.
In honor of Eugene Debs. In honor of Emma Goldman.

THREE TEARS

1

If you have seen a single yellow iris
standing watch beside the garden,
then you have seen the Major General weeping
at four in the morning in his mother's Bible;
and if you have seen the rows and rows of onions,
then you have seen the army with its shoes half off
and its rifles half stacked and half scattered in the witch hazel.
But you who have seen the half-eaten leaves of the hackberry
have seen the saddest sight of all,
a nest inside a ruined building,
a father hugging his child,
a Jew in Vilna.

2

You would have to sit at my bedroom window
to see the dog of hay guarding the strawberries.
He is twice the size of an Irish wolfhound
and heavier than a bear.
He belongs to the hairy species with the sheepdog
and the long-nosed collie.
He lies there day after day in the middle of the garden
with his paws crossed under his chin and his eyes watching the road.
He is so clean-smelling and so peaceful
that we forget the strength in his huge body
and the malice in his jaws.

3

I have to lie on my back for two hours
before a certain cloud comes by;
then I only have three or four good seconds
before it disappears again for another day.
What would it have been like
if there had been no maples and no viburnum
to cut off my vision,
if I could have lived all year in the sand
with nothing to stop me but my own thoughts,
if I could have let my eye go freely down the line
choosing its own movement and its own light?

LUCKY LIFE

Lucky life isn't one long string of horrors
and there are moments of peace, and pleasure, as I lie in between the
   blows.
Lucky I don't have to wake up in Phillipsburg, New Jersey,
on the hill overlooking Union Square or the hill overlooking
Kuebler Brewery or the hill overlooking SS. Philip and James
but have my own hills and my own vistas to come back to.

Each year I go down to the island I add
one more year to the darkness;
and though I sit up with my dear friends
trying to separate the one year from the other,
this one from the last, that one from the former,
another from another,
after a while they all get lumped together,
the year we walked to Holgate,
the year our shoes got washed away,
the year it rained,
the year my tooth brought misery to us all.

This year was a crisis. I knew it when we pulled
the car onto the sand and looked for the key.
I knew it when we walked up the outside steps
and opened the hot icebox and began the struggle
with swollen drawers and I knew it when we laid out
the sheets and separated the clothes into piles
and I knew it when we made our first rush onto
the beach and I knew it when we finally sat
on the porch with coffee cups shaking in our hands.

My dream is I'm walking through Phillipsburg, New Jersey,
and I'm lost on South Main Street. I am trying to tell,
by memory, which statue of Christopher Columbus
I have to look for, the one with him slumped over
and lost in weariness or the one with him
vaguely guiding the way with a cross and globe in
one hand and a compass in the other.
My dream is I'm in the Eagle Hotel on Chamber Street
sitting at the oak bar, listening to two
obese veterans discussing Hawaii in 1942,

and reading the funny signs over the bottles.
My dream is I sleep upstairs over the honey locust
and sit on the side porch overlooking the stone culvert
with a whole new set of friends, mostly old and humorless.

Dear waves, what will you do for me this year?
Will you drown out my scream?
Will you let me rise through the fog?
Will you fill me with that old salt feeling?
Will you let me take my long steps in the cold sand?
Will you let me lie on the white bedspread and study
the black clouds with the blue holes in them?
Will you let me see the rusty trees and the old monoplanes one more
     year?
Will you still let me draw my sacred figures
and move the kites and the birds around with my dark mind?

Lucky life is like this. Lucky there is an ocean to come to.
Lucky you can judge yourself in this water.
Lucky you can be purified over and over again.
Lucky there is the same cleanliness for everyone.
Lucky life is like that. Lucky life. Oh lucky life.
Oh lucky lucky life. Lucky life.

MALAGUEÑA

With a dead turtle floating down my canal
and a stone pillar in my river
and wild jewels growing outside my door,
all I have to do is reach up
and I am back again, living with shadows.

I come from such an odd place
that the slightest wind ignites me
and the smallest tremor makes me weep or lie down.

Tonight, in the dark living room, my daughter is
playing "Malagueña" on her warped piano.
After two weeks of dampness the moist notes
float across the road trying to find brotherhood
with anything that is crooked or twisted or smiling.

I am over here in the garage
letting the mold take over;
I am getting ready for my own
darkness;
I am letting the sound of the islands
go through my veins again, like water.

PILE OF FEATHERS

This time there was no beak,
no little bloody head, no bony
claw, no loose wing—only a small
pile of feathers without substance or center.

Our cats dig through the leaves, they
stare at each other in surprise,
they look carefully over their shoulders,
they touch the same feathers over and over.

They have been totally cheated of the body.
The body with its veins and its fat
and its red bones has escaped them.
Like weak giants
they try to turn elsewhere.
Like Americans on the Ganges,
their long legs twisted in embarrassment,
their knees scraping the stones,
they begin crawling after the spirit.

GOLD FLOWER

This is the season for chrysanthemums,
the gold flower of Japan.
Everything else is already spotted and dry and crumbled.
I am holding five varieties in my hand,
the quill, the daisy, the spoon, the spider, the button.
I am putting them in clean jars and glasses.
I didn't begin my new worship
until the last sun of the year
brought me face to face with the shiny clusters.
I had never seen them before.
I had walked through gardens all my life without seeing them.
How ignorant I was;
and what I lost through anger and impatience.
Dear ladies, how gravely you stand there in your wool suits and your
      jewelry;
what strength there is in your fingers;
how you have come to resemble each other after twenty years.
Dear old man, how your great nose and your pouches took over at
      last;
how your hand hangs limply over its pipe;
how you smile in the middle of your bright giants
remembering your dead wife.
Dear world of strangers!
Dear life I half missed!
Oh dear religions and cultures.
Dear hidden rules. Dear hidden men and women
carrying the sunlight down into the soft dirt with you.

HONEY LOCUST

Here are about seventy snakes waiting to come to life,
each one about a foot long,
with noisy seeds inside them like little coffee beans.

They are curled up for the winter,
some in the leaves, some on the grass walk,
some lying face down or face up in the snow.

I put about twenty in my pocket so I can look at them
when I get home and tear them apart slowly
and shake them like old rattles in my ear.

I read and study all night trying to understand their cries
as they pull themselves loose and dance around in their beds
and sing about their lives like old musicians
singing about theirs.

GERT'S GIFTS

There were two jokes played on me on my first long walk in Florida
    this winter,
the English muffin joke and the foam rubber joke.
Nothing else fooled me, none of the grotesqueries and combinations,
not even the driftwood tree growing fresh purple flowers on its
    green tips.
It's good to be back in Florida where the dead things bloom,
where the sea grapes drop leather leaves in the sand
and the saw grass grows through the cracked cement
and the sweet honeys walk by on silk platforms
promising luxury and renewal in the green darkness.

STEPPING OUT OF POETRY

What would you give for one of the old yellow streetcars
rocking toward you again through the thick snow?

What would you give for the feeling of joy as you climbed
up the three iron steps and took your place by the cold window?

Oh, what would you give to pick up your stack of books
and walk down the icy path in front of the library?

What would you give for your dream
to be as clear and simple as it was then
in the dark afternoons, at the old scarred tables?

LOVE FOR THE DOG

Before he opened his eyes, as he lay there under the window,
he was convinced he would be able to speak this time and sort
    things out
clearly as he did when his tongue was still a hammer;
a half hour later he was once again on the chair
with all these keepers staring at him in pity and fear
and giving him milk and cocoa and white napkins.
In the middle of his exhausted brain there rose a metaphor
of an animal, a dog with a broken spine sliding around
helplessly in the center of the slippery floor
with loving owners all around encouraging him
and the dog trying desperately to please them.
He sat there proud of his metaphor, tears of mercy in his eyes,
unable in his dumbness to explain his pleasure,
unable now even to rise because of the spine.
He felt only love for the dog,
all different from the ugly muscular cat
which had leaped the day before on his bony thigh
as if it were a tree limb or an empty chair,
as if he could not run again if he had to,
as if there was not life still pouring out voluptuously
like wild water through all his troubled veins.

THIS IS IT

It is my emotions that carry me through Lambertville, New Jersey,
sheer feeling—and an obscure detour—that brings me to a coffee shop
called "This Is It" and a small New Jersey clapboard
with a charming fake sign announcing it to be
the first condemned building in the United States
and an old obese collie sitting on the cement steps
of the front porch begging forgiveness with his red eyes.
I talk to the coughing lady for five minutes,
admire her sign, her antique flag, her dog,
and share her grief over the loss of the house next door,
boarded up forever, tied up in estates,
surrounded by grass, doomed to an early fire.

Everyone is into my myth! The whole countryside
is studying weeds, collecting sadness, dreaming
of odd connections and no place more than Lambertville
will do for ghosts to go through your body
or people to live out their lives with a blurred vision.
The old woman is still talking. She tells me
about her youth, she tells me about her mother's ganglia
and how the doctor slammed a heavy Bible down
on her watery wrist, scattering spoons and bread crumbs
and turning over little tin containers
of alyssum and snapdragon. She tells me about the
curved green glass that is gone forever. She tells me
about her dog and its monotonous existence.

Ah, but for sadness there are very few towns like Lambertville.
It drips with grief, it almost sags from the weight.
I know Frackville, Pa., and Sandusky, Ohio,
and I know coal chutes, empty stores and rusty rivers
but Lambertville is special, it is a wooden stage set,
a dream-ridden carcass where people live out serious lives
with other people's secrets, trying to touch with their hands
and eat with their cold forks, and open houses with their keys;
and sometimes, on a damp Sunday, they leave the papers on the front
      porch
to walk down York Street or Buttonwood Street
past abandoned factories and wooden garages,
past the cannon with balls and the new band shell,

past the downtown churches and the antique shops,
and even across the metal plates on the Delaware River
to stinking New Hope, where all their deep longing
is reduced to an hour and a half of greedy buying.

I crawl across the street to have my coffee at the low counter,
to listen to the noise of the saws drifting through the open window
and to study the strange spirit of this tar paper cafe
stuck on a residential street three or four blocks
from Main and Bridge where except for the sudden windfall
of the looping detour it would be relegated forever
to the quiet company of three or four close friends
and the unexpected attention of a bored crossing guard
or exhausted meter man or truck driver.
I listen to the plans of the three teen-age businessmen
about to make their fortune in this rotting shack
and walk—periodically—past the stainless steel sink
to take my piss in the misplaced men's room.
I watch the bright happy girls organize their futures
over and around the silent muscular boys
and I wait, like a peaceful man, hours on end,
for the truck out back to start, for the collie to die,
for the flies to come, for the summer to bring its reckoning.

THE CEMETERY OF ORANGE TREES
IN CRETE

In Crete the old orange trees are cut back until they are stumps,
with little leaves coming out again from the butchered arms.
They are painted white and stand there in long straight rows
like the white gravestones at Gettysburg and Manassas.
    I first came across them on the bus ride to Omalos
as we began our climb through the empty mountains,
thinking of the beauty and exhaustion that lay ahead.
They are mementos of my journey south, the renewal
of my youth, green leaves growing out of my neck,
my shoulders flowering again with small blossoms,
my body painted white, my hands joining
the other hands on the hill, my white heart remembering
the violence and sorrow that gave us our life again.

96 VANDAM

I am going to carry my bed into New York City tonight
complete with dangling sheets and ripped blankets;
I am going to push it across three dark highways
or coast along under 600,000 faint stars.
I want to have it with me so I don't have to beg
for too much shelter from my weak and exhausted friends.
I want to be as close as possible to my pillow
in case a dream or a fantasy should pass by.
I want to fall asleep on my own fire escape
and wake up dazed and hungry
to the sound of garbage grinding in the street below
and the smell of coffee cooking in the window above.

IF YOU FORGET THE GERMANS

If you forget the Germans climbing up and down the Acropolis,
then I will forget the poet falling through his rotten floor in New
    Brunswick;
and if you stop telling me about your civilization in 1400 B.C.,
then I will stop telling you about mine in 1750 and 1820 and 1935;
and if you stop throwing your old walls and your stone stairs at me,
then I will drop my overstuffed chairs and my rusty scooters.
—Here is an old leather shoe to look at;
give me anything, a pebble from the Agora, a tile from Phaistos;
and here is a perfectly intact bottle of Bollo;
give me a delicate red poppy or a purple thistle growing beside the
    Parthenon.
Here are the photographs, myself crawling out on the charred beam,
a carton of Salems, a crib with mattress, a pigeon feather,
a plywood door, a piece of the blue sky,
a bottle of Smirnoff's, a bottle of Seagram's,
a bottle of Night Train Express.
Show me yours, the oldest theater in Europe,
a woman playing the harp, a marble foot,
a bronze frying pan, a fish swimming in crystal,
a boar's tusk helmet, a god screaming, a painted eyelid.
Here are the thoughts I have had;
here are the people I have talked to and worn out;
here are the stops in my throat;
here is the ocean throwing up dead crabs and card tables.
—If you go by bus, take the Suburban Transit
and get off if you can before the Highland Park Bridge.
If you go by car, take route 18 east
past the Riverview Bar and try to park
on either Peace or Church.
If you walk, go north on Church past the old Gramercy
and the health food store and God's Deliverance Center
to the mound of dirt and the broken telephone booth.
Do not bury yourself outright in the litter;
walk gently over the broken glass;
admire the pictures on the upstairs rear wall.
Sing and cry and kiss in the ruined dining room
in front of the mirror, in the plush car seat,

a 1949 or '50, still clean and perfect
under the black dust and the newspapers,
as it was when we cruised back and forth all night looking for
    happiness;
as it was when we lay down and loved in the old darkness.

THE HUNGARIAN

If I waited till September
I could no longer walk on the bottom of the river.
I would be up to my waist in water,
fighting off gnats
and trying to find the stones with my soggy shoes.
By then the Hungarian would already be back in Europe,
telling his friends about the man he met in Pennsylvania
who spoke to him in German and told him about the
glaciers and the violent American poison.
—I could have kissed him goodbye, I knew him so well.
We walked up and down the mule path for two hours
with our hands behind us.
We bent down to pick up fish hooks and cigarette packs
as if we were walking through our own park.
We touched in each other one last loving time
the dream of justice we both had buried in our own rivers
like two gnostics who buried their city's statues
twenty feet down in the thick mud and the shadows
to keep them from greed and hatred,
to save them for the serious souls to come.

BOB SUMMERS: THE FINAL POEM

There are two men I know who wander around all winter as I do,
half listening and half falling over rocks and curbs.
One is a bicyclist who pedals all day on
an old balloon-tire bike through Upper Black Eddy;
the other is a bridge-walker who wears a long army
overcoat with "P.O.W." still faintly printed across the back.
There was a third who walked down the streets of Philadelphia,
touching base at the Chess Club and Frank's and the Greek's
like a farmer, or beggar, doing the daily round.
If you saw just the back of his head
and his hands waving you would know he was leading you
through one of his darker arguments;
if you followed him further
you would be dragged to a place where every connection was smashed
and the brain had trouble sorting out its own riches.
I last saw him concentrating with all his power
on the problem of simple existence,
trying to match words with places
and blurred thoughts with things,
reducing everyone who knew him or came near him
to a state of either pity or shame
because of his strangeness and clumsiness.
I remember the rope he carried
and the knot of terror he fingered as he daydreamed,
the knot of release, hanging slack like a crown
over the back of his neck,
always ready to guide him through his weakness,
ready to give him back his health and wisdom.

GOD OF RAIN, GOD OF WATER

Each spring the long-nosed god of rain,
when it's his turn, rises from the gang of old men
sitting day and night in the dirt in front of the fire
and makes the monotonous noises and does the slow
crawling steps and little bows that are his stock in trade.
Tears pour from his eyes, rheum from his nose,
saliva from his mouth and clean colorless water
in an endless cascade from his swollen tube.

I see him in various conventional shapes in the clouds,
long arms slowly shifting through the light and dark,
or sometimes in the leaves of the two trees,
waving his head and shoulders in the sky
and dropping mist on everything that passes,
or sometimes as an all-night and all-day rain
filling the whole house with dread and sorrow,
or sometimes just as a dirty runnel sweeping
relentlessly through stones and leaves and paper
and down the storm sewers to the river,
singing wildly in the underground passages.

What I do is go around the countryside looking for mosses
or wait for the geese to come back up the river
or stare at the strange red blossoms in my front yard
that are either old seedpods or new leaves on the old maples.
There is a line of sticks I look at on the Jersey side
that I can just see from my bedroom window before my own
trees turn green and blot out the view.
When these sticks grow soft, when there's a slight blur on everything,
then I know the bees are circling the dead logs,
the vines are taking hold in the new dirt
and the first flowers are starting to use the light.

Then I remember other springs
when, in a sudden fit of violence, my own life was changed
in the very middle of its flowering.
I am able to zero in on those years with more clarity now
as each new one passes, so that not one detail is lost;
as if the clarity illuminated the pain;
as if the pain decreased where the clarity took over;

as if the clarity were taking the place of the pain.
—The old man when he goes back into the circle is still weeping
and War and Procreation and Music, three of the oldest and saddest,
slap him on his soaking back, shouting above the roar of the fire
and the constant din of the unorganized gods chattering,
"Nice show, good show, good show," but he, the rain god,
is sobbing uncontrollably, thick drops are coming from his eyes,
and he is gasping and finally his arms alone are moving,
and he is in the center of the huge circle on his hands and knees
pounding the earth, dry gasps are coming from his throat
and a trickle of thin water from his mouth,
while all around him violets are springing up in the dirty cinders,
and giant thistles and strings of chicory and daisies,
to pay him for his tears, to pay the old god for his tears,
apart from everything else, to pay him for his tears.

IF YOU SAW ME WALKING

If you saw me walking one more time on the island
you would know how much the end of August meant to me;

and if you saw me singing as I slid over the wet stones
you would know I was carrying the secret of life in my hip pocket.

If my lips moved too much
you would follow one step behind to protect me;

if I fell asleep too soon
you would cover me in light catalpa or dry willow.

Oh if I wore a brace you would help me, if I stuttered
you would hold my arm, if my heart beat with fear

you would throw a board across the channel, you would put
out a hand to catch me, you would carry me on your back.

If you saw me swim back and forth through the algae
you would know how much I love the trees floating under me;

and if you saw me hold my leaf up to the sun
you would know I was still looking for my roots;

and if you saw me burning wood
you would know I was trying to remember the smell of maple.

If I rushed down the road buttoning my blue shirt—
if I left without coffee—if I forgot my chewed-up pen—

you would know there was one more day of happiness
before the water rose again for another year.

MORNING HARVEST

Pennsylvania spiders
not only stretch their silk between the limbs
of our great trees but hang between our houses
and pull their sheets across the frantic eyes
of cats and the soft chests of men.
Some are so huge they move around like mammals,
waddling slowly over the rough cement
and into the bushes to nurse their young or feed
on berries and crunch on bones.
But it is the ones that live on the iron bridge
going across to Riegelsville, New Jersey,
that are the most artistic and luxurious.
They make their webs between the iron uprights
and hang them out in the dew above the river
like a series of new designs on display,
waiting for you to choose the one most delicate,
waiting for you just to touch the sticky threads
as you look at their soft silk, as you love them.

If your mind is already on business,
even if your mind is still into your dream,
you will be shocked by their beauty and you will sit there
two minutes, two hours, a half a century you will sit there
until the guards begin to shout, until they rush up in confusion
and bang on your window and look at you in fear.
You will point with your left finger at the sun
and draw a tracery in the cold air,
a dragline from door handle to door handle,
foundation lines inside the windows,
long radials from the panel to the headrest
and gluey spirals turning on the radials;
and you will sit in the center of your web
like a rolled-up leaf or a piece of silent dirt,
pulling gently on your loose trapline.
They will scream in your ear,
they will tear desperately at the sheets,
they will beg for air
before you finally relieve them by starting your engine
and moving reluctantly over the small bridge.

Do not regret your little bout with life in the morning.
If you drive slowly you can have almost one minute
to study the drops of silver hanging in the sun
before you turn the corner past the gatehouse
and down the road beside the railroad cars
and finally over the tracks and up the hill
to the morning that lies in front of you like one more design.
It is the morning I live in and travel through,
the morning of children standing in the driveways,
of mothers wrapping their quilted coats around them
and yellow buses flashing their lights like berserk police cars.
It is lights that save us, lights that light the way,
blue lights rushing in to help the wretched,
red lights carrying twenty pounds of oxygen down the highway,
white lights entering the old Phoenician channels
bringing language and mathematics and religion into the darkness.

PEDDLER'S VILLAGE

The small gray bird that fit inside the hand
of a nine-year-old girl is himself a grandfather
with a tear stuck to the side of his round face;

but he hopped on the red bricks and absentmindedly
pecked at her hand as if he were still young and blue,
with oily wings and a stomach full of seeds.

If she could see his heart she would know how terrified he was.
She would take off her colored handkerchief and stop being his
        grandmother;
she would take away his paper bed and stop being his sister and his
        bride.

If she knew how old he was she would bow down
and kiss his loose feathers
and listen carefully to his song.

There had to be wisdom with all that age,
something he could give her,
something she could remember him by and love him for;

there had to be some honor, some revelation,
some loveliness before he died;
before the lice robbed him,
before the bitter wire snapped him in two,
before a thousand tragedies took away his warmth and happiness.

THE SWEETNESS OF LIFE

After the heavy rain we were able to tell about the mushrooms,
which ones made us sick, which ones had the dry bitterness,
which ones caused stomach pains and dizziness and hallucinations.

It was the beginning of religion again—on the river—
all the battles and ecstasies and persecutions
taking place beside the hackberries and the fallen locust.

I sat there like a lunatic,
weeping, raving, standing on my head, living
in three and four and five places at once.

I sat there letting the wild and domestic combine,
finally accepting the sweetness of life,
on my own mushy log,
in the white and spotted moonlight.

UNDERGROUND DANCING

There's a bird pecking at the fat;
there's a dead tree covered with snow;
there's a truck dropping cinders on the slippery highway.

There's life in my backyard—
black wings beating on the branches,
greedy eyes watching,
mouths screaming and fighting over the greasy ball.

There's a mole singing hallelujah.
Close the rotten doors!
Let everyone go blind!
Let everyone be buried in his own litter.

SOMETHING NEW

This year I sat with women, gathering up
wet sand between my legs and making Byzantine
castles with my gritty hands. It was the first time
in four years I didn't dream up
a new encounter with a black cloud or a ruined building
to describe the state of my mind. I sat there
discussing the simple pleasures, beekeeping
and massage, poker and ice-cream making,
as well as the more serious matters
such as divorce and bladder infection, and I thought
only of the harmony between us and the love
that would last forever by the boring sea.
Forgive me ten times, but this is what I did, and
except for the brutal argument over middle-income housing
between myself and the fat stomach sitting next to me
there was nothing but peace and affection in our little community.
Yes, on the third day, at three o'clock,
I noticed that the sky dropped and the ground lost its weight,
but that was only because a storm was coming up and
the air currents seemed to make the earth move more quickly.
Everybody got cold and began shaking out sheets
or started climbing the hill toward the houses
but nobody saw any sudden warning or important anniversary out
      there.
For that matter we all returned the next day
and began another castle and buried combs and love notes
in the sand and drank Diet Pepsi and
ate pieces of raw cauliflower with sand giblets in them.
Next summer is the charm and already
I am getting ready for it; I am waiting
for the shore and the ocean to stop their sloppy maneuvering
for one minute; I am waiting for my body
to slow down and my mind to stop falling apart
every other year like a cheap clock; I am imagining
what the waves will look like this time when I am finally standing
on the black rocks with another whole year behind me,
and I am imagining myself whispering words of greeting—
"Kalimera, kalimera"—to the little Greek genius
inside the hill of sand that used to be our castle
and her looking up with unforgiving eyes,

daring me to give myself up to the waves as she did,
daring me to simplify my twisted feelings
and throw away this and throw away that and live
as she does under the buried notes and the combs,
singing and humming and sleeping by the sea she loves.

III | THE RED COAL

1981

COW WORSHIP

I love the cows best when they are a few feet away
from my dining-room window and my pine floor,
when they reach in to kiss me with their wet
mouths and their white noses.
I love them when they walk over the garbage cans
and across the cellar doors,
over the sidewalk and through the metal chairs
and the birdseed.
—Let me reach out through the thin curtains
and feel the warm air of May.
It is the temperature of the whole galaxy,
all the bright clouds and clusters,
beasts and heroes,
glittering singers and isolated thinkers
at pasture.

THE FACES I LOVE

Once and for all I will lie down here like a dead man,
letting the socialists walk over my face, letting the fascists
crawl through my veins, letting the Krishnas
poison me with their terrible saffron.

Once and for all I will lie here helpless and exhausted.
I will let dishonor rise from me like steam
and tears fall down on me like oily rain.

In the end my stillness will save me;
in the end the leopard will walk away from me in boredom
and trot after something living, something violent
and warm to excite him before his death.

In the end I will have my own chair.
I will pull the blinds down and watch my nose and mouth
in the blistered glass.
I will look back in amazement at what I did
and cry aloud for two more years, for four more years,
just to remember the faces, just to recall the names,
to put them back together—
the names I can't forget, the faces I love.

LITTLE WHITE SISTER

It was in Philadelphia that I first lived a life of deferment,
putting everything off until I could be at ease.
There, more than in New York and more than in Paris,
I lay for hours in bed, forgetting to eat, forgetting
to swim, dying of imperfection and loneliness.
It was in Vienna that I learned what it would be like
to live in two lives, and learned to wander between them;
and it was in the rotten underbelly
of western Pennsylvania that I was saved twice by a pear tree,
one time living and one time dead, and enslaved
once and for all by a patented iron grate
carrying words of terror through the yellow air.
    My ear betrayed me, my little white sister
glued to the side of my head, a shiny snail
twisted everywhere to catch the slightest
murmur of love, the smallest sobbing and breathing.
It wasn't the heart, stuck inside the chest
like a bloody bird, and it wasn't the brain,
dying itself from love; it was that messenger,
laughing as she whispered the soft words,
making kissing sounds with her red lips,
moaning with pleasure for the last indignity.

IMMENSITY

Nothing is too small for my sarcasm. I know
a tiny moth that crawls over the rug
like an English spy sneaking through the Blue Forest,
and I know a Frenchman that hangs on the closet door
singing *chanson* after *chanson* with his smashed thighs.
I will examine my life through curled threads
and short straws and little drops of food.
I will crawl around with my tongue out, growing
more and more used to the dirty webs hanging
between the ridges of my radiator and the huge
smudges in that distant sky up there, beginning
more and more to take on the shape of some great design.
   This is the way to achieve immensity, and this is the
only way to get ready for death, no matter what Immanuel Kant
and the English philosophers say about the mind,
no matter what the gnostics say, crawling
through their vile blue, sneezing madly in the midst of that
life of theirs, weighed down by madness and sorrow.

ROTTEN ANGEL

My friends, still of this world, follow me to the bottom of the river,
tripping over roots and cutting themselves on the dry grass.
They are all over on the left side, drinking beer and crying,
and I am there by myself waiting for the rotten angel.
For my sake it hasn't rained for twenty days
and all the old jetties are showing up again in the water.
I can reach my arms up into the second row of branches
and pull down clumps of dead leaves and barrel hoops.
I finally find my clearing and fall down in the dirt,
exhausted from thirty minutes of fighting for air.
I put an x on the ground and start marking off
a place for the gravel, the rhododendron and the iron bird.
My friends stand above me, a little bored by my death
and a little tired of the flies and the sad ritual.
—How I would love it if I could really be buried here,
a mile away from my house in this soft soil.
I think the state could do this for me—they could give me
a few feet of earth—they could make an exception.
I tell you it really matters and all that talk
about so many cents' worth of fat and so many grams
of water is really just fake humility.
I would hate being dusted on the ocean or put in a drawer
for perpetuity—I want to be connected
with life as long as possible, I want to disappear slowly,
as gruesome as that sounds, so there is time
for those who want to see me in my own light
and get an idea of how I made my connections
and what I looked at and dreamed about
and what the river smelled like from this island
and how the grackles sounded when they landed
in the polished trees and how the trucks sounded
charging up 611 carrying the culture
of Philadelphia into the mountains
and how the angel must have gasped as he swam
back to the shore and how he must have dipped
his head in the green water to escape the gnats
swarming after him in the dirty sunlight
a million miles from his New York and his Baltimore and his Boston.

PICK AND POKE

I began this fall by watching a thin red squirrel
sneak out of my neighbor's wrecked Simca and run over
a pile of bricks into one of its small forests.
Then and there I set up my watch
so I could follow that sweet redness
in and out of our civilization.
     It would have been so easy with the old English taxi
at Pick and Poke. It stands six feet high,
like a small coach waiting for its shabby prince
to walk through his porch posts and his barrels
and mount the leather seat in two short steps,
whereas the Simca is practically buried in the leaves,
its glass is gone, and half its insides are rotted.
But it isn't size, and it isn't even location;
it has something to do with character, and something
to do with ideas, and something, even, to do
with the secret history of France, and of England.
After two weeks I saw everything
as clearly as a squirrel does—a Simca
is part of nature, lying halfway between
the wet maples and the field of tarpaulin,
the armrest is a perch, the back seat is a warehouse,
and the gearshift is a small dangerous limb.
But my loyalty is mostly to England,
so I found myself wandering down
day after day to the big yard at Pick and Poke.
There I studied the square wheelbarrow
and the lawn furniture—I walked around the taxi,
measuring the giant wheels and fancy tool box,
and I sat in the back and rapped on the glass partition
over the jump seats, ordering my driver to carry me
down the river to New Hope and Philadelphia.
After just a few hours I understood the English spirit,
and after a day I even understood the English garden
from watching the scattered shutters and old storm windows.
     We here in France salute the English.
We admire them for their tolerance and shyness.
We love them for their geography and their music,
their hatred of theory and their bad food,
their optimism and love of animals.

We in America are more like red squirrels: we live
from roof to roof, our minds are fixed on the great
store of the future, our bodies are worn out from leaping;
we are weary of each other's faces, each other's dreams.
We sigh for some understanding, some surcease,
some permanence, as we move from tree to tree,
from wire to wire, from empty hole to empty hole,
singing, singing, always singing, of that amorous summer.

ROYAL MANOR ROAD

It would be worth it to go ninety miles out of your way
to see these cows eat and sleep and nuzzle in the mud.
It would be worth it to leave the tables at Grand Ticino
and walk down Thompson Street talking about the eyes—
"Are they the eyes of Kora, are they soft and slanted;
are they the eyes of Juno and drunken Hathor?"
All my reading, all my difficult reading
would be worth it as I stood in the weeds
watching them run up like kittens, watching them
crowd each other for little tastes of clover and hepatica.
To reach my hand inside
and touch the bony forehead and the stiff hair
would be worth it.

MODERN LOVE

In a month all these frozen waterfalls
will be replaced by Dutchman's breeches
and I will drive down the road
trying to remember what it was like
in late February and early March.
It will be 72 degrees on March 24th
and I will see my first robin
on the roof of the Indian Rock Inn.
My wife and I will go in to stare at the chandelier
and eat, like starved birds, in front of the fireplace.
I know now that what I'll do
all through supper is plan my walk
from Bristol, Pa., to the canal museum.
I will exhaust her with questions about old hotels
and how much water I should carry
and what shoes I should wear,
and she will meet me with sweetness and logic
before we break up over money and grammar and lost love.
Later the full moon will shine through our windshield
as we zigzag up the river
dragging our tired brains, and our hearts, after us.
I will go to bed thinking of George Meredith
lying beside a red sword
and I will try to remember how his brain smoked
as he talked to his wife in her sleep and twisted her words.
   Where I will go in the six hours before I wake up freezing
I don't know, but I do know
I will finally lie there with my twelve organs in place,
wishing I were in a tea palace, wishing
I were in a museum in France, wishing
I were in a Moorish movie house in Los Angeles.
I will walk downstairs singing because it is March 25th
and I will walk outside to drink my coffee on the stone wall.
There will still be drops of snow on the side of the hill
as we plant our peas and sweep away the birdseed.
Watch me dig and you will see me
dream about justice, and you will see me
dream about small animals, and you will see me
dream about warm strawberries.
From time to time I will look over

and watch her dragging sticks and broken branches
across the road. We are getting ready
for summer. We are working in the cold
getting ready. Only thirty more days and the moon
will shine on us again as we drive to Hellertown
to see Jane Fonda grimace, and drive back
after midnight through the white fields,
looking for foxes in the stubble,
looking for their wild eyes, burning with fear and shyness,
in the stunted remains of last summer's silk forest.

LITTLE DID THE JUNCO KNOW

Little did the junco know who he was keeping company with this
    Christmas,
he and the nuthatch and the chickadee and the red sparrow,
racing back and forth between the bag of fat
and the pan of birdseed under the dead vine.

Little did those sweethearts know who was in their midst,
with his round eye and his small head and his plump body
rolling after the neck like a mop keeping up with its tiny handle.

And little did he know himself why people fought over him
and waved him in the air and sent him out
morning after morning in the first light—
that soft gray one with the long tail
and the monotonous voice,
gorging himself at the battered aluminum pan.

LORD, FORGIVE A SPIRIT

So what shall we do about this angel,
growing dizzy every time he climbs a ladder,
crying over his old poems.
I walk out into the garden and there he is,
watering the lilies and studying the digitalis.
He is talking to his own invisible heart;
he is leaking blood.
    The sun shines on him all day long
as he wanders from bush to bush.
His eyes flash with fire, his eyelashes blaze and
his skin shines like brass,
but he trips in the dirt just like any gardener, or grieving poet.
    I watch him walk beside the cactus;
I watch him kneel in front of the wet horsetails;
I touch his lips.
I write all day. I sit beside him all
day long and write the garbled words.
I sit in the sun and fill a whole new book
with scrawls and symbols.
I watch the sky as he talks about the gold leaf
and the half-forgotten ruins; I watch the words
drift from his mouth like clouds.
I watch the colors change from orange to red
to pink as he tries to remember his old words—
his old songs, his first human songs—
lost somewhere in the broken glass and the cinders,
a foot below the soft nails and the hinges.

ELAINE COMPARONE

I love to sit down
in front of my lilac fence
and watch the wind blow through the pointed leaves.

If I could do exactly what I wanted
I would move a harpsichord into my back yard
and ask Elaine Comparone to play for me all morning.

My friend Barbara Dazzle said she would move
her dining-room furniture out and put the long red box
in the middle of the gardenias and the hanging ivy.

Either way I would listen to the steel bird sing
and watch Elaine shift back and forth on her chair,
torn between my love of Domenico Scarlatti
and my desire to lay my head down on her flowery lap.

My joy begins as I dream of a woman blushing
beside her stone wall, and my pain begins
when she turns into a shadow, with notes falling
around her like blossoms on the wet grass.

I run through the garden shouting kiss me, kiss me!
In one more day the petals will be curled and brown,
they will lie piled up like dead leaves—
smeared on the walk like blood;

oh in one hour the great tree will stand there shaking
and the box will be carried out like a heavy coffin
and Elaine Comparone will sit with her hands in her lap,
in the cold air, rushing back to the city,
remembering the notes falling on the ground
and the red spikes inside the creamy blossoms
and the new leaves making their way like tiny crescendos
in the drawing rooms of Petrograd and Stockholm,
dreaming of sunlight and rain and endless dancing.

I REMEMBER GALILEO

I remember Galileo describing the mind
as a piece of paper blown around by the wind,
and I loved the sight of it sticking to a tree
or jumping into the back seat of a car,
and for years I watched paper leap through my cities;
but yesterday I saw the mind was a squirrel caught crossing
Route 80 between the wheels of a giant truck,
dancing back and forth like a thin leaf,
or a frightened string, for only two seconds living
on the white concrete before he got away,
his life shortened by all that terror, his head
jerking, his yellow teeth ground down to dust.

It was the speed of the squirrel and his lowness to the ground,
his great purpose and the alertness of his dancing,
that showed me the difference between him and paper.
Paper will do in theory, when there is time
to sit back in a metal chair and study shadows;
but for this life I need a squirrel,
his clawed feet spread, his whole soul quivering,
the hot wind rushing through his hair,
the loud noise shaking him from head to tail.
    O philosophical mind, O mind of paper, I need a squirrel
finishing his wild dash across the highway,
rushing up his green ungoverned hillside.

MAGRITTE DANCING

Every night I have to go to bed twice,
once by myself, suddenly tired and angry,
and once when my wife turns the weak light on
and stumbles over my shoes into the bathroom.
Some nights there is a third time—the phone
is ringing and I rush out into the hall;
my heart is pounding but nobody is there
and I have to go back to bed empty-handed
just as my brain was beginning to pick up signals.
This time it takes me all night to get back to sleep.
I don't sink again into the heavy pillow
but lie there breathing, trying to push
everything back into its own channel.
For hours I watch the dark and then gradually
I begin watching the light; by that time
I am thinking again about snow tires and I am thinking
about downtown Pittsburgh and I am thinking
about the turtles swimming inside their brown willows.
I look at the morning with relief, with something close
to pleasure that I still have one more day,
and I dance the dance of brotherliness and courtliness
as first my neighbor the postman, pocked and pitted,
goes crawling off in his early morning bitterness
and then my neighbor the body man goes bouncing away,
his own car rusty and chromeless, his T-shirt torn,
his eyes already happy from his first soothing beer.
    The dance I dance is to the tune of Magritte
banging his bedposts on a square mountain,
and Oskar Schlemmer floating up a stairway,
and Pablo Picasso looking inside a woman's head.
I dance on the road and on the river and
in the wet garden, all the time living in Crete
and pre-war Poland and outer Zimbabwe,
as through my fingers and my sparkling hair
the morning passes, first the three loud calls
of the bluejay, then the white door slamming,
then the voices rising and falling in sudden harmony.

THE SHIRT POEM

It is ten years since I have seen these shirts
screaming from their hangers, crying for blood and money.
They shake their empty arms
and grow stiff as they wait for the light to come.
I open the door an inch at a time to let them out
and start candles all over the room to soothe them.
—Gone is sweetness in that closet, gone is the dream
of brotherhood, the affectionate meeting
of thinkers and workers inside a rented hall.
Gone are the folding chairs, gone forever
the sacred locking of elbows under the two flags.

On Sunday night they used to sing for hours
before the speeches. Once the rabbis joined them
and religion and economics were finally combined in exile.
"Death is a defect," they sang, and threw their hats
on the floor. "We will save nature from death,"
they shouted, and ended up dancing on the small stage,
the dark crows and the speckled doves finally arm in arm.

They will never come back—in a thousand years;
it is not like bringing a forest back, putting a truckload
of nitrogen in the soil, burning some brush,
planting seedlings, measuring distance—
these are people, whose secret habits we no longer know,
how they tore their bread and what designs they made on the
        tablecloth,
what they thought about as they stared through the warped glass,
what the melting ice meant to them.

Poor dead ones! Forgive me for the peace I feel as I walk out
to the mailbox. Forgive me for the rich life I lead.
Forgive me for the enormous budget and the bureaucracy and the
        permanent army.
When I come home from New York City I stand outside
for twenty minutes and look out at the lights.
Upstairs the shirts are howling and snapping,
marching back and forth in front of the silver radiator.
In a minute I will be up there closing doors
and turning on lamps.

I will take the papers out of my coat pocket
and put them in their slots.
I will think of you with your own papers and your rubber bands.
What is my life if not a substitute for yours,
and my dream a substitute for your dream?
Lord, how it has changed, how we have
made ourselves strange, how embarrassing the words
sound to us, how clumsy and half-hearted we are.

I want to write it down before it's forgotten,
how we lived, what we believed in;
most of all to remember the giants
and how they walked, always with white hair,
always with long white hair hanging down over their collars,
always with red faces, always bowing and listening,
their heads floating as they moved through the small crowd.

Outside the wind is blowing
and the snow is piling up against the pillars.
I could go back in a minute to the synagogue in Beechview
or the Carnegie Library on the North Side.
I could turn and shake hands with the tiny man
sitting beside me and wish him peace.
I could stand in front and watch the stained-glass
window rattle in its frame and the guest speaker
climb into the back seat of his car.

I am writing about the past because there was
still affection left then, and other sorrows;
because I believed my white silk scarf could save me,
and my all-day walks;
because when I opened my window the smell
of snow made me tremble with pleasure;
because I was a head taller than the tiny man sitting next to me;
because I was always the youngest;
because I believed in Shelley;
because I carried my entire memory along with me in the summer;
because I stared at the old men with loving eyes;
because I studied their fallen shoulders and their huge hands;
because I found relief only in my drawings;
because I knew the color and texture of every rug and every chair
and every lampshade in my first house.

Give this to Rabbi Kook who always arrived
with his clothes on fire and stood between the mourners,

singing songs against death in all three languages
at the crowded wall, in the dark sunlight.

And give this to Malatesta who believed in
the perfect world and lived in it as he moved
from country to country, for sixty years, tasting the
bread, tasting the meat, always working,
cursing the Church, cursing the State,
seeing through everything, always seeing the heart
and what it wanted, the beautiful cramped heart.

My shirts are fine. They dance
by themselves along the river
and bleed a little as they fall down on the dirty glass.
If they had knees they would try to
crawl back up the hill and stop the trucks
or march back and forth singing their swamp songs.
They see me coming and fly up to the roof;
they are like prehistoric birds,
half leaping, half sailing by.
They scream with cold, they break through the hall window
and knock over baskets and push open doors
until they stand there in place, in back of the neckties,
beside the cold plaster, in the dust
above the abandoned shoes, weeping in silence,
moaning in exhaustion,
getting ready again to live in darkness.

JUNE FIRST

FOR ABIGAIL THOMAS

Some blossoms are so white and luscious, when they
hold their long thin hands up you strip them for love
and scatter them on the ground as you walk;

and some birds look at you as if there were no
great line drawn between their lives and yours,
as if you drank together from the same cement;

and some pods spin in the wind as if you would not pick
them up gingerly to see if they had wings
and then would not break them open to see what made them
fall, to study their visceras.

I touch you as I would the sawdust in the eaves
or the crazy buttercups in the middle of the mulepath
or the frightening foil
jumping and leaping in front of the oily grackles;

and I touch you as I touch the grass, my body falls down on the
        ground
and I pull at the roots as I watch you in the limbs
bending down to avoid the red blossoms,
hiding in the leaves,
reaching up like the tallest dryad,
your curved arms and your jeweled fingers
waving slowly again in the hot sun.

THINKING ABOUT SHELLEY

Arm over arm I swam out into the rain,
across from the cedars and the rickety conveyor.
I had the quarry all to myself again,
even the path down to the muddy bank.
Every poet in the world was dead but me.
Yeats was dead, Victor Hugo was dead,
Cavafy was dead—with every kick I shot
a jet of water into the air—you could see
me coming a mile away, my shoulders rolling
the way my father's did. I started moving
out into the open between the two islands,
thinking about Shelley and his milky body.
No one had been here before—I was the first
poet to swim in this water—I would be the
mystery, I would be the source
for all the others to come. The rivers of China
were full of poets, the lakes of Finland, the ponds
of southern France, but no one in Pennsylvania
had swum like this across an empty quarry.
I remember at the end I turned on my back
to give my neck a rest; I remember floating
into the weeds and letting my shoulders touch
the greasy stones; I remember lying
on the coarse sand reaching up for air.
    This happened in June before the berries were out,
before the loosestrife covered the hills, before
the local sinners took off their clothes and waded
like huge birds in the cold water.
It was the first warm day and I was
laboring in this small sea.
I remember how I hoped my luck would last;
I remember the terror of the middle
and how I suddenly relaxed after passing the islands;
I remember it was because of Shelley
that I changed my innocent swim
into such a struggle,
that it was because of Shelley
I dragged my body up, tired and alive,
to the small landing under the flowering highway,
full of silence now and clarity.

JOSEPH POCKETS

Have you ever lived through seven fat years and grown soft
from eating lamb and bulgur? I remember lawyers
standing in line for doughnuts and geniuses painting
the walls of Idlewild Airport. Two things happened
to make me remember: one was a film about the 30s,
put together to show the times as primitive
in the Eisenstein style; the other was my invasion
of Kaufmann's department store to buy a suit
from the crowd of salesmen dressed up in plaids and
              stripes,
to go with my new dignity and ferocity.

In *The Hunger March* thousands of lean men converge
on Washington in sheepskin coats and fedoras.
Already the cap was dead; already the workingmen
had started to move out of their small houses.
The joy was watching them go through city after city.
The joy was watching the camera catch their happiness
as they half ran down the old highways,
singing of empty stomachs and freezing rain.

In *The Ford Massacre* the figures move
in a rush across the screen; they either are buried
down the tracks in puffs of smoke or stand
on top of you, screaming for justice in silent voices.

The seven lean years came first—they lasted seven years;
the seven fat years lasted over twenty-five.
Joseph comes later. He turns the past into a dream
and shows us how we lived and what disappeared
as we left the 40s and went into the 50s.
I'm back in Pittsburgh now; it's only here
and maybe Detroit and maybe a little Chicago
that there are Joseph pockets where you can see
the dream turned around and the darkness illuminated,
some of the joy explained, some of the madness—
Chicago, St. Louis, Minneapolis, Boston, Buffalo.

When I walked into the lobby I felt like a visitor.
I sat beside a black-haired woman with a shawl

who knew what I was radiating and touched me
on the little wooden arm. I lived in a Joseph
pocket there and when I left she touched me
again as if to say, "Well, wait for me. The marches
will be over in fifteen minutes and we can walk
through Father Demo Square past our brick mansion
where we could imagine living in half-dark rooms,
drinking tea from flowered cups and sleeping
in modern anarchy under the blue skylight."

When I walked into Kaufmann's I carried the past
with me like a colored stone in my pocket.
Two diplomats walked over, their eyes showing
almost no pity, their voices cold and resentful
as they abandoned me in front of the hooded sweaters.
I had to look at suits myself; I had to learn
about European cuts and what vents did for my body
and what my sloping shoulders needed and where the
sleeves should end and where the collar should be,
without a sucking salesman hanging on
and dragging me around from rack to rack.

I will be living in Pittsburgh one more month.
All the time I am here I will move between
my hatred of Frick and my love of the forty bridges.
Over and over again I will walk downtown
through Market Square and past the Oyster House,
or I will drive through South Side and Mt. Washington
wishing the Japanese could see these hills.
This is the city where art was brought in by the trainload
and Mellon money is wasted to bring Grace Kelly
on stage to read poems about birds and their transcendence.
This is the city where Iron is our drink, we say, "Iron,"
we say, "Give me Iron," we say, "Piss on watery Miller's."
This is the city where I lay down like a twisted
poppy to read my Marlowe and my Pound.

I can look down the river from my back room.
It's worth a million dollars. I can see
the lights hanging from broomsticks and the cars
bouncing up and down on the crooked boulevard.
But the best view is ten o'clock in the morning;
the sun is behind me then and I can see
the light shining down on the whole city.
I want to float on that river—what dark legs

will push me, what silk hand will carry me
across the plain to the first row of mountains,
or drop me, singing, into the other river
beside a coal barge or a sleek cruiser?

My sister is buried in Carrick in the Jewish cemetery
three miles from the Liberty Tubes, beside my grandmother,
Libby Barach, and my grandfather, B. Barach,
both of them resting above her like two old friends.
For once I feel cut off and except for the presence
of the blue Nova in front of the service building
I might be in a Jewish graveyard in Poland,
crowded with souls, everyone a stranger.

I borrow a book from the bleak office and open
to the page to be read at the graveside of a sister.
I ask her first to remember her shocking death
and all the clumsiness and sadness of her leaving.
I ask her to describe—as she remembers it—
how I stood in front of her white coffin
and stared at the mourners in our small living room.
I ask her to think again about the two peach trees,
how close together they were, how tiny their fruit was,
forty years ago in the light rain,
wherever she is, whatever sweet wing she's under.

This is my last Joseph pocket. I am going
back to New York City. O Japanese,
you will love this place; you will spend a week
visiting junk stores and eating steaks and buying
boots and dishes to take with you back to Asia.
What I'll do is talk to the glass buildings
and explain myself. I think I'll stand in one place
to say good-by. I think I'll leave in the snow
with the wind blowing down the alley and the cars
going ten miles an hour up the Parkway, the cinder trucks
moving along in convoys, big clouds of steam
rising up from the river, all the sorrows
of life disappearing like drops of snow
as we pick up speed going east on the empty turnpike.

DAYS OF 1978

This is the only thing that clarifies my life,
this beautiful old living room
with the pink walls and the mohair sofa.
I walk out every night singing
a little song from Gus Williams or W. C. Handy.
I throw my yellow scarf around my neck
and pull my cap down over my eyes.
Even here I am dressed up,
walking through the light flakes and the ice puddles.
—Tonight I will think about Cavafy
and the way he wept on his satin pillow,
remembering the days of 1903.
I will compare my life to his:
the sorrows of Alexandria,
the lights on the river;
the dead kings returning to Syria,
the soap in my bath.
—Later I will lie on my own pillow
with the window open and the blinds up,
weeping a little myself at the thick blankets
and the smoking candles
and the stack of books,
a new sweetness and clarity beginning
to monopolize my own memory.

NO WIND

Today I am sitting outside the Dutch Castle
on Route 30 near Bird in Hand and Blue Ball,
watching the Amish snap their suspenders at the sunglasses.
I am dreaming of my black suit again
and the store in Paradise where I will be fitted out for life.
    A small girl and I recognize each other
from our former life together in Córdoba.
We weep over the plastic tote bags, the apple combs and the laughing
      harmonicas,
and fall down on the hot carpet
remembering the marble forest
of the Great Mosque
and the milky walls
of the Jewish quarter.
    I will see her again in 800 years
when all this is sorted out.
I give it that much time,
based on the slack mind,
the dirty drinking water and the slow decay.
I give it at least that much time
before we lie down again in the tiny lilacs
and paper love houses of the next age.

THE ANGEL POEM

My broken wing is on the left near the large joint
that separates me so crazily from half the others.
I think of trees and how they break apart
in the wind, how sometimes a huge branch
will hang in strips, what would be skin
in humans or angels, and how the flesh
is like pulp, and almost blood-red where the break is.

I tend to drag the wing because the pain
in lifting it is too much for me to stand.
That part of me that is still human recalls
what pain in the shoulder can be, and I remember
not only the sharp stabs when I had to turn
but the stiffness that made me keep my arm at my side
and forced me to plan my eating and my sad sleeping.

As far as birds, I am more like a pigeon than a hawk.
I think I am one of those snow-white pigeons with gold
eyes and a candy-corn beak, with a ruffled
neck—a huge white hood—and ruffled
legs, like flowers or long white pantaloons,
shamelessly exposed under my white dress
and hopelessly drooping when I run in
fear and slip and fall on the dirty newspapers.
I fly with shame, when I fly, but mostly I sit
quietly or rise with effort to do my dance,
my head moving back and forth like a loose pendulum.

My main thought is how I can translate pain
into a form that I can understand,
so I break a wing or bruise my foot; but the wound
is more like panic, more like flying
without a shadow or flying in darkness,
something like the human dream when fear
makes them rise out of a sound sleep
and move without control above their bodies,
along the ceiling or through the closed windows,
pushing and yelling as they fall through the glass.
Either way we both have bloody feathers and
wake up groggy, sitting on the foot of the bed

listening to the birds slow down and the day start,
thinking about the dream and its double meaning.

I have looked myself up in the Jefferson Market Library,
in the pink basement where the ghosts of hundreds
of coiners and draft dodgers are still standing
under the arches, waiting to be dragged away.
Sometimes I sit there for hours reading about winged
servants and the mountains of justice and
the hierarchies of the Moors and the Akkadians.
I know—if anything—I am one of the million
Enoch encountered on his first trip to Heaven.
I sit against a freezing wall—my place is
forever against a freezing wall—my hands
hanging loosely down from my knees, a black cat
of Heaven rubbing up against my leg.
I know I am also the dark part of the leaf,
that I walk upright, that I am half snow, half fire,
that I can move like light from one end of the house to the other,
that I have something in common with Tammuz, and with Shelley.

I am wearing my long gray coat so I can hide
whatever I have to inside like stiff parchment.
I walk upstairs to look at the stained-glass windows
and touch the yellow stars and ruby petals
or move along the shelves, reaching at random
for the literature that will change my life.
I love this library above all others—I love
the two stone heads and the huge painted doors,
and I love standing outside underneath the pillars
and the great carved seal of New York City,
with all that Bavarian madness above me,
the clock and the chimneys and the turrets and the gargoyles,
a step away from the drowned lion on
one side and the fenced-in Greening on the other.
I wait for fifteen minutes, helping couples
move their heavy strollers, telling time
to Temple blonds dragging their sacred books,
and talking sweetly to Vichians and Spinozists.
Across the street is Balducci's where lamb chops go
for thirty dollars a pound and salmon is guarded
by Cuban soldiers; and just up Sixth is the flower
store, loaded with carnations and chrysanthemums,
where I was taken for a city inspector
with my yellow tablet and my blue jacket.

I start my walk at seven o'clock. Maybe
I'll reach the Port Authority by eight-thirty or nine.
All those who live in pain go on fixed walks
between two stations and mark the passage with drops
of blood. They push against each other, bruising
their delicate shoulders and legs—who would know
that one man's stomach is gone, that one has ankles
the size of balloons, that one is in terror
of impotence, that one has blood in her throat.
Dreiser is there pitying the dying poor,
Dostoevsky is studying the black sky,
Balzac is making new souls out of the dust.
They wear wings over their leather coats
and walk through mud as I walk over cement
and shout at the horses blocking their narrow paths.
When I reach Fourteenth I am practically running—past
the Greenwich Savings Bank and Corby's Bar,
past the dead pigeon and the Vitamin Quota.
I start to sing at Eighteenth Street across
from Wanamaker's lost department store—a kind
of Parthenon in the heart of the old soft goods—
and make my turn at Twenty-third past the empty
Paradise Cafeteria. I stop, lovingly
and longingly, in the lobby of the Chelsea
to look at the marble and dream about my life
as a man of letters, coming down the elevator
and standing outside in front of the bronze plaques
before I go to the nearest Blarney Stone
to eat my stew and think about my future.

On Eighth Avenue I am joined by the others
and we make our way down our own Dolorosa
like chirping grasshoppers and gurgling pigeons.
At ten to eight we walk into the empty lobby
of the New Yorker to look at the Moonie squads
and stop our music as we enter the corridor—
the six blocks between Thirty-fourth and Fortieth—
filled with every charm from disco centers
to cheap clothes to Spanish groceries;
adult book stores and movies and topless dancers;
readers and advisers; pimps and baby whores.
We set up headquarters beside the Trailways
in competition with the Children of Love,
but music is illegal at the Port Authority
so we put down our combs and potatoes

and walk away—like the others—with crushed vision.
—I have one hope, that we can leave together
by one of the upper gates and come slowly
into Sea Isle City or Asbury Park,
piping our souls away, singing all day
with no constraints—no bus drivers, no policemen,
no music teachers or critics or wise widows—
in French and Italian, Greek if we want to, or Slovak,
hymns and love songs, ballads and madrigals,
rattling the windows and shaking the sweet highways.

I think the sea and the sea air will mend
my stiff arm; I know that I will float
for hours in the icy water, humming
my new poems; I know that when the others
go, like mist, or gray jelly, or tiny crabs,
I will lie on the sand and make my own imprint,
seven or eight feet this time, a giant
sand angel, with footprints like a bear's,
with delicate hair, oh delicate hair on the brown
hill, and deep holes where my elbows are,
and little shivery markings where I turned
and moved my arms up and down through the soft valleys.

I will stay only long enough to watch one child—or two—
discover the image and run up to the iron benches
shouting, "An angel, an angel, there was an angel lying
on our beach; he was ten feet tall and his wings
were curved at the top like the white bird at school.
We saw him fly over the old Imperial,
then bounce on top of the huge red tiles
and bow—like a drunk—to the dancing whale,"
before I walk down to the yellow bus station
and buy my ticket at the frosted window
for Easton, Pennsylvania, or New York, New York.

VISITING FLORIDA AGAIN

At Eleventh and Euclid I stood in front of an air
conditioner and listened to it whir. For just a second
I thought it was an insect screaming in anger
before it sucked up its enemy or ran into the hibiscus
to brood. For the first time
I gave thanks to my brother the machine,
my little friend, so out of place in the tropics,
so close now, compared to the hideous ichneumon
waving its long needle
or the velvet ant
searching for babies—
so misunderstood and abused.
—Shivering in the heat, I wanted to touch
some great yellow steam shovel or biplane,
something so oily and awkward
that it coughed and groaned for hours
before it moved its huge body
into position.
I felt as pure as Mayakovski
climbing into his aluminum vest,
as dear as Pico della Mirandola
watching his Jewish soul rise.
I joined the Shakers at their sweet stations,
the Anarchists
resting in the sun.
For just one second I was in London again
in the iron palace,
I was in Pittsburgh,
sitting in the old reference room,
reading Thomas Paine and William Blake and Peter Kropotkin,
creating my first dreams.

JUNE FOURTH

Today as I ride down Twenty-fifth Street I smell honeysuckle
rising from Shell and Victor Balata and K-Diner.
The goddess of sweet memory is there
staggering over fruit and drinking old blossoms.
A man in white socks and a blue T-shirt
is sitting on the grass outside Bethlehem Steel
eating lunch and dreaming.
Before he walks back inside he will be changed.
He will remember when he stands again under the dirty windows
a moment of great misgiving and puzzlement
just before sweetness ruined him and thinking
tore him apart. He will remember lying
on his left elbow studying the sky,
and the loss he felt, and the sudden freedom,
the mixture of pain and pleasure—terror and hope—
what he calls "honeysuckle."

HANGING SCROLL

I have come back to Princeton three days in a row
to look at the brown sparrow in the apple branch.
That way I can get back in touch with the Chinese
after thirty years of silence and paranoid reproach.
It was painted seven hundred years ago by a Southerner
who was struggling to combine imitation and expression,
but nowhere is there a sense that calligraphy
has won the day, or anything lifeless or abstract.
I carry it around with me on a post card,
the bird in the center, the giant green leaves
surrounding the bird, the apples almost invisible,
their color and position chosen for obscurity—
somehow the sizes all out of whack, the leaves
too large, the bird too small, too rigid,
too enshrined for such a natural setting,
although this only comes slowly to mind
after many hours of concentration.

On my tree there are six starlings sitting and watching
with their heads in the air and their short tails under the twigs.
They are just faint shapes against a background of fog,
moving in and out of my small windows
as endless versions of the state of darkness.
The tree they are in is practically dead,
making it difficult for me to make plans
for my own seven hundred years
as far as critical position, or permanence.
—If the hanging scroll signifies a state
of balance, a state almost of tension
between a man and nature or a man and his dream,
then my starlings signify the tremendous
delicacy of life and the tenuousness of attachment.
This may sound too literary—too German—
but, for me, everything hangs in the balance
in the movement of those birds,
just as, in my painter,
his life may have been hanging from the invisible apple
or the stiff tail feathers or the minuscule feet.
I don't mean to say that my survival
depends upon the artistic rendering;

I mean that my one chance for happiness
depends on wind and strange loyalty and a little bark,
which I think about and watch and agonize over
day and night,
like a worried spirit
waiting for love.

A HUNDRED YEARS FROM NOW

A hundred years from now nobody will know who Zane Grey was
nor what the ten-cent pulp smelled like
nor what it was like to carry *Liberty* magazines on your back.
If you are bored to death by this then think of Wallace Stevens
when he first walked into the University of Pennsylvania library
and the memories he had of certain leather chairs,
or think of Ts'ai Yen in the land of frost and snow,
remembering his sweet mother.

I myself am searching for the purple sage that I can share
for all time with the poets of Akkadia and Sumeria.
I am starting with my river bottom, the twisted
sycamores and the big-leaved catalpas, making the connections
that will put Zane Grey in the right channel. I am
watching a very ancient Babylonian who looks something
like me or Allen Ginsberg before he shaved his beard off
pick up *The Border Legion* and *The Riders of the Trail*
from the dust. I am explaining him the spirit
of America behind our banality, our devotion
to the ugly and our suicidal urges;
how Zane Grey, once he saw the desert,
could not stop giving his life to it,
in spite of his dull imagination and stilted prose;
how the eternal is also here,
only the way to it is brutal.
O Babylonian, I am swimming in the deep off the island
of my own death and birth. Stay with me!

THE POEM OF LIBERATION

The smell of piss is what we have in the city
to remind us of the country and its dark ammonia.
In the subway it's like a patch of new lilac
or viburnum in the air or like that pocket
of cold water you swim in at Batsto
or that other pocket of water at Amagansett.
In the telephones it sinks in the metal plates
like the smell in a rug or a rotten sofa,
a stain you run away from in grief and anger.

Sometimes I walk in the East Side past the brownstones
on Fifty-second Street or the long sleek canopies
that almost cover the sidewalks from Fifth to Madison.
Then it's like remembering the stone walls in Italy
or the tiny alleys behind the bazaars in Africa.
Then I know, walking in front of Park East
or the Hampton House or the Penguin,
that New York will be the first city to go,
and we will no longer live like English,
hating the sight of sweet bananas and thick-armed
women smashing dice against the boards.

Across the street from St. John's there is a large
vegetable garden planted in the rubble
of a wrecked apartment house, as if to claim
the spirit back before it could be buried
in another investment of glass and cement.
There are thin maples and pieces of orange brick
and weeds and garbage as well as little rows
of beans and lettuce and hills of squash and melons.
It is a confused garden but I think the
soul of New York is there in the vague balance
of shape against shape and in the lush presence
of objects, from the blue cement fish pond
to the curved brick walk to the outdoor grille and chair;
a boxed-in mulch pit, iron candelabra, deep
irrigation ditches, delicate flower beds,
everything crowded into the smallest space.

I stand on the steps in front of the straining prophet,
looking across at the other two buildings, saved
by the squatters in 1970. I look at the splintered
doors and the pile of rubbish outside the windows
and make my own philosophical connections.
Behind the church, totally hidden from the street,
is another garden, planted by the women
of St. John's, this one a biblical
fantasy of trees and herbs and flowers,
from Matthew and John and Samuel, laid out in perfect
clusters, poplar from Genesis, reeds from Kings,
nettles from Job, lovely carob from Luke,
completely different from the other garden,
but not a mirror image of it
and not a sacred version of the profane,
one a vile parody of the other,
although these ideas flooded through my mind.

I fall asleep under the olive trees
thinking of Jezebel and Elijah.
I want to like one garden and hate the other
but I find myself loving both, both ideas,
both deeply thought out, both passionate.
I talk to the fat Englishman—the curator
of the church museum—about the two gardens
and the squatters and the church's benign role
and get his views on property, and mercy,
and study his tiny feet and row of books.
Finally I walk across the street again
to look at the People's Garden and plan my
little corner next to the climbing roses,
maybe a hosta or a bleeding heart.

My last hour is spent reading the poem
of liberation—in Spanish and English—
nailed up on the wire fence
and walking through the Plaza Caribe
under the slogans and the brown faces.
—At first I think it's hope again, hope played out
on a two-stringed instrument or a soggy drum.
Hebrew melancholy and Moorish wailing
under a fringed lamp, in a ruined chair,
but then I realize it's hope mixed in with memory
and not that other bitter stupid dream again,
stuck to the face like a drop of baby dew.

I love memory too, the weeping mouth
that will not let you go, the sweet smell drifting
through the alleys, the hum at the high window;
and I love the fact that, this time, no one will stand
with his straw hat in his hand in the marble courtroom
singing, "I love you, Kate Smith. I love you, I love you,
I love you, *presidente*, I love you, *señor* mayor."
I dig a hole in the ground
and pour in my mixture of meal and water.
I spread the roots out in three directions
and pack them in with dirt.
I leave by the southern gate
across the street from the Hungarian pastry
and walk down 111th like a Bedouin farmer,
like a Polish shepherd,
like a Korean rope master,
my small steel shovel
humming and singing in the blue dust.

ACACIA

In locust trees the roots run along the ground
and bury themselves in the sides of hills for survival.
They grow in roses and strawberries
and come from little sticks humbly and touchingly.
In three counties I am the only one who loves them;
I am the only one who reads about them in Ilick;
I am the only one who grieves when they turn brown and
die, or lie bent and broken in the rain.

Three summers ago I walked through the streets of Albi
with my friend Dave Burrows—who has since become Das Anudas—
and a French parasite and his little American wife.
We saw the locusts from the river not far from the brick
cathedral—made out of Protestant blood—not far from the huge
Toulouse-Lautrec collection housed in a palace,
something, it seemed to me then, like housing hundreds
of baby lambs or tons of fresh flowers
in the lobby or restaurant of a Howard Johnson's.

We argued for half an hour about the locust.
He told me it was now French but originally
it grew in southern China and India.
I told him it came from western Pennsylvania
and was brought to Europe in the nineteenth century.
He told me it was planted on the side of streets and in parks
because of its shade and its ornamental qualities.
I told him it was practically a weed in America,
that farmers valued it mainly for fence posts.

I remember his wife—she was displaced;
her eyes were round, her skin almost transparent.
We ate a late supper in the square near the railroad
station and her voice had already assumed that
flat ungoverned tone I have heard in dozens
of museums and restaurants from London to Heraklion.
When she and I talked English her vile husband
frowned and barked at her in his southern French,
and when I shook hands with her to say good-by
and kissed her on the side of her small mouth
it was like stripping those tiny leaves from their stems

or smelling again the sweetest of all blossoms,
like being again in the Allegheny mountains
where locusts first started, four million years ago.

And that, my love, is a continent and a half away
from Albi, where the northern French descended
on the southern French and in the name of Jesus
destroyed their culture and their strange religion
and made them build a tributary cathedral
where Das Anudas and I walked all morning,
noting every detail of the pink fortress,
fainting from the beauty,
growing hungry from the climb,
changed forever halfway through our lives.

YOUR ANIMAL

The final end of all but purified souls
is to be swallowed up by Leviathan,
or to be bound with fiery chains and flogged
with 70 stripes of fire.
I walk along the mule path dreaming of my weaknesses
and praying to the ducks for forgiveness.
Oh there is so much shit in the universe
and my walks, like yours,
are more and more slippery and dangerous.
I love a duck for being almost like a vegetable.
I love him because his whole body can be consumed,
because there is no distance between him and his watery offal.
Your animal is almost human,
distant from his waste,
struggling to overcome the hated matter,
looking up with horrified white eyes,
eternally hunting for space in the little islands of Riverside Drive
and the fenced-in parks of the Village.

I love duck and potatoes, duck and red beets,
duck and orange juice.
I love the head of duck dipped in sugar,
I love chocolate duck with chipolota sausages,
fragrant crisp duck mixed with shrimp and pork.
I love the webs and the heart; I love the eggs
preserved in lime and potash, completely boned duck
filled with ham and chestnuts, fried duck with pineapple
and canned red cherries or sections of tangerine.

This is a poem against gnosticism;
it is a poem against the hatred of the flesh
and all the vicious twists and turns we take
to calm our frightened souls.
It is a poem celebrating the eating of duck
and all that goes with it.
It is a poem I am able to write after walking every day
through the flocks, and loving the babies, and watching them slip
down the mud sides and float into the current.
It is a poem about shooting galleries and cardboard heads,
about hunters and their checkered hats and frozen fingers,

about snow-white cloths and steaming laced-up birds
and waiters standing in little regiments
getting ready to run in among the tables and start carving.
—It is my poem against the starving heart.
It is my victory over meanness.

THE ROSE WAREHOUSE

Ah tunnel cows,
watching over my goings out
and my comings in,
you preside, like me, over your own butchery.

I always look for you
when I go back to Pennsylvania,
driving under the rusty piers
and up Fortieth Street.

All of New York must be laid out for you up there,
the slope on Park Avenue,
the moon on the river,
the roof of the Port Authority.

I feel like putting up my own head,
the head of Gerald Stern,
on the side of the Rose Warehouse, his glasses slipping off,
his tears falling one by one on Eleventh Avenue.

I want to see if he will sing
or if he will stare out at the blue sky forever and forever.
I want to see if he's a god
and feels like murmuring a little in the lost tongue

or if he's one of those black humans,
still mourning after thirty years—
some German Jew
talking about Berlin,

the town that had everything;
some man of love
who dug his own grave and entered there;
some sorrowful husband

refusing to wash, refusing to listen to music,
cutting his flesh, rubbing dust in his hair,
throwing in dirt, throwing in flowers,
kissing the shovel good-by, kissing the small shovel.

THE RED COAL

Sometimes I sit in my blue chair trying to remember
what it was like in the spring of 1950
before the burning coal entered my life.

I study my red hand under the faucet, the left one
below the grease line consisting of four feminine angels
and one crooked broken masculine one

and the right one lying on top of the white porcelain
with skin wrinkled up like a chicken's
beside the razor and the silver tap.

I didn't live in Paris for nothing and walk
with Jack Gilbert down the wide sidewalks
thinking of Hart Crane and Apollinaire

and I didn't save the picture of the two of us
moving through a crowd of stiff Frenchmen
and put it beside the one of Pound and Williams

unless I wanted to see what coals had done
to their lives too. I say it with vast affection,
wanting desperately to know what the two of them

talked about when they lived in Pennsylvania
and what they talked about at St. Elizabeth's
fifty years later, looking into the sun,

40,000 wrinkles between them,
the suffering finally taking over their lives.
I think of Gilbert all the time now, what

we said on our long walks in Pittsburgh, how
lucky we were to live in New York, how strange
his great fame was and my obscurity,

how we now carry the future with us, knowing
every small vein and every elaboration.
The coal has taken over, the red coal

is burning between us and we are at its mercy—
as if a power is finally dominating
the two of us; as if we're huddled up

watching the black smoke and the ashes;
as if knowledge is what we needed and now
we have that knowledge. Now we have that knowledge.

The tears are different—though I hate to speak
for him—the tears are what we bring back to the
darkness, what we are left with after our

own escape, what, all along, the red coal had
in store for us as we moved softly,
either whistling or singing, either listening or reasoning,

on the gray sidewalks and the green ocean;
in the cars and the kitchens and the bookstores;
in the crowded restaurants, in the empty woods and libraries.

THERE IS WIND, THERE ARE MATCHES

A thousand times I have sat in restaurant windows,
through mopping after mopping, letting the ammonia clear
my brain and the music from the kitchens
ruin my heart. I have sat there hiding
my feelings from my neighbors, blowing smoke
carefully into the ceiling, or after I gave
that up, smiling over my empty plate
like a tired wolf. Today I am sitting again
at the long marble table at Horn and Hardart's,
drinking my coffee and eating my burnt scrapple.
This is the last place left and everyone here
knows it; if the lights were turned down, if the
heat were turned off, if the banging of dishes stopped,
we would all go on, at least for a while, but then
we would drift off one by one toward Locust or Pine.
—I feel this place is like a birch forest
about to go; there is wind, there are matches, there is snow,
and it has been dark and dry for hundreds of years.
I look at the chandelier waving in the glass
and the sticky sugar and the wet spoon.
I take my handkerchief out for the sake of the seven
years we spent in Philadelphia and the
steps we sat on and the tiny patches of lawn.
I believe now more than I ever did before
in my first poems and more and more I feel
that nothing was wasted, that the freezing nights
were not a waste, that the long dull walks and
the boredom, and the secret pity, were
not a waste. I leave the paper sitting,
front page up, beside the cold coffee,
on top of the sugar, on top of the wet spoon,
on top of the grease. I was born for one thing,
and I can leave this place without bitterness
and start my walk down Broad Street past the churches
and the tiny parking lots and the thrift stores.
There was enough justice, and there was enough wisdom,
although it would take the rest of my life—the next
two hundred years—to understand and explain it;

and there was enough time and there was enough affection
even if I did tear my tongue
begging the world for one more empty room
and one more window with clean glass
to let the light in on my last frenzy.
—I do the crow walking clumsily over his meat,
I do the child sitting for his dessert,
I do the poet asleep at his table,
waiting for the sun to light up his forehead.
I suddenly remember every ruined life,
every betrayal, every desolation,
as I walk past Tasker toward the city of Baltimore,
banging my pencil on the iron fences,
whistling Bach and Muczynski through the closed blinds.

WAVING GOOD-BY

I wanted to know what it was like before we
had voices and before we had bare fingers and before we
had minds to move us through our actions
and tears to help us over our feelings,
so I drove my daughter through the snow to meet her friend
and filled her car with suitcases and hugged her
as an animal would, pressing my forehead against her,
walking in circles, moaning, touching her cheek,
and turned my head after them as an animal would,
watching helplessly as they drove over the ruts,
her smiling face and her small hand just visible
over the giant pillows and coat hangers
as they made their turn into the empty highway.

DEAR MOLE

Dear mole, I have forgotten you!
Living under the dahlias, making highways
under the pines, coming up to sniff
blindly, like John Ruskin,
at the pink chrysanthemums and the red berries
hanging from the ruined viburnum.

Everything depends on your sponginess,
the world you created with your
shoulders and claws,
the long tunnels and the quiet rooms
where you can wander—like Ruskin—
dreaming of smooth floors and vaulted ceilings.

He was like you,
always cramming and ramming, spluttering in disgust,
hating repression, living apart from others,
adoring mountains, drifting with the vortices,
hemorrhaging a little,
loving high sounds, loving the crystal orders.

He was like you,
following the laws of the fourteenth century,
envious of the fish,
curiously breathless and obsessed with shadows,
loving small girls, living deep in Hell,
always beginning, always starting over,
his head down, his poor soul warbling and wailing.

ARTHUR'S LILY

I could never feel sorry for Arthur Vogelsang,
resting among his kafir-lilies and his phoenix tree.
I could never say there he is
in Los Angeles wiping his eyes from the smog
and leaping across the great crack in his sidewalk.
He has a whole desert to live in without poets;
he has the letter of Ezra Pound cursing jellyfish;
he has the city of Baltimore to remember.
—I could never drop a tear for him,
knowing he is standing by his crooked mailbox;
I could never lure him with our warm water
or touch him with our snow,
knowing he is buying a white Chrysler,
knowing he is throwing the grapefruit;
I could never drag him back,
knowing he is talking to the cement frog,
knowing he is practicing footprints,
knowing he is planning another ecstatic voyage.

THE PICASSO POEM

It was when the bridal wreaths were all out
and those smelly weeds, the graduation speakers,
were blooming on one green lawn after another
that I sat on my porch trying to make up my mind
about the Pablo Picasso I loved the most.
It was Sunday morning and the *New York Times*
was full of his glory; it was Sunday
and the skinny runners were out
and the iris were combing their tiny beards
and the lilacs were waving a dark good-bye.
I wanted to drive a 1936 Pontiac
to New York City to see the exhibition.
I wanted to drive through sweet New Jersey with the picnic
basket bumping my knee and the line of trees
keeping the sun out from Phillipsburg to Newark.
Over and over again I thought of him
in the 1930s and I thought of the paintings
he did and I thought of the France he loved,
all plump and modern and corrupt.
He was 55 in 1936 and slipping
through the silence before his next flowering;
he was moving from one hard place to another,
dipping his hand and smearing the white canvas.
—I think I'd have to choose between the woman
with a hat or the one with rope for a face
or the one reclining—with stars—or the one in a nightmare
ripping apart a handkerchief;
or maybe the goat; or maybe the bicycle handle.
    On June ninth I stood peacefully in line
waiting to crawl through the numbered rooms.
I was so quiet little birds were resting
on my soft shoulder and little leaves were growing
from my legs and arms.
Somewhere, inside my chest, a heart was pounding,
and I was listening again, a little thinner
and a little whiter than the last time.
I walked through the birches, I walked through the dry rain,
I bent down and ran my fingers
through the black dirt. Three hours from then
I would walk down that line from the other side,

dreaming—I think—of my own next darkness.
God save Fifth Avenue, God save New York
from my assault. God let me drive
across the Pulaski Skyway singing those great
songs; leaning out the little window
and staring down at the Jersey swamp;
smelling that sulphur; driving up into the sun
and looking back on those iron lamps; looking forward
over and over to the future, streets in the sky,
towers in the ground, dancing people, little
dogs for every family. I waver between
that world and this. I travel back and forth
between the two. I lose myself
and crawl off singing or come back crying,
my face wet with misery, my eyes deep holes
where the dream was lost, my hands up in their favorite
position, the two unbroken fingers
cutting the air,
thirty feet above the river,
beside the hostas and the mugho pine,
the dirty bottles and the stones
fixing the boundary for another summer.

THE ROAR

That was the last time I would walk up those five
flights with a woman in tow, standing
in the hall patiently trying my keys,
listening to my heart pounding from the climb.

And the last time I would sit in front of the
          refrigerator, drinking white wine and asking
questions, and lecturing—like a spider—
and rubbing my hand through my hair—like a priest.

Look at me touch the burning candle
with my bare palm and press a rusty knife
against my left eyelid while she undresses.

Look at me rise through the cool airshaft
and snore at the foot of the bed with one hand
on her knee and one hand touching the white floor,

the red and blue beacon of Empire
just beyond those little houses
as familiar now as my crippled birch

and the endless roar out there
as sweet as my own roar
in my other dream, on the cold and empty river.

FOR NIGHT TO COME

I am giving instructions to my monkey
on how to plant a pine tree. I am telling
him to water the ground for hours before
he starts to dig and I am showing him
how to twist the roots so the limbs will bend
in the right direction.
                              He is weeping
because of the sweet air, and remembering
our canoe trip, and how we went swimming
on Mother's Day. And I am remembering
the holiness and how we stopped talking
after we left Route 30. I show him the tree
with the two forks and the one with the
stubs and the one with the orange moss
underneath, and we make our nest in a clearing
where the wind makes hissing noises and the sun
goes through our heavy clothes.
                                    All morning we lie
on our backs, holding hands, listening to birds,
and making little ant hills in the sand.
He shakes a little, maybe from the cold,
maybe a little from memory,
maybe from dread. I think we are lost,
only a hundred yards from the highway,
and we will have to walk around in fear,
or separate and look for signs before
we find it again.
                        We pick a small green tree,
thick with needles and cones and dangling roots,
and put it in the trunk on top of the blanket,
and straighten the branches out, and smooth the hairs.
All the way back we will be teary and helpless,
loving each other in the late afternoon,
and only when we have made the first cut
and done the dance
and poured in the two bushels of humus
and the four buckets of water
and mixed it in with dirt and tramped it all down
and arranged and rearranged the branches
will we lie back and listen to the chimes

and stop our shaking
and close our eyes a little
and wait for night to come
so we can watch the stars together,
like the good souls we are,
a hairy man and a beast
hugging each other in the white grass.

HERE I AM WALKING

Here I am walking between Ocean and Neptune,
sinking my feet in mile after mile of wet life.
I am practically invisible
in the face of all this clutter,
either straying near the benches over the buried T-shirts
or downhill in the graveyard
where the burned families are sleeping in the sun
or eating dry lunch among the corpses.
I will finish walking in two hours
and eat my sandwich in the little park
beside the iron Methodist.
This is the first step.
Tomorrow I will start again in Barnegat
and make my way toward Holgate or Ventnor.
This is something different
than it was even five years ago.
I have a second past to rake over
and search through—another 2,000 miles of seashore
to account for.
—I am still making my mind up
between one of those art deco hotels
in Miami Beach, a little back room on a court
where you could almost be in Cuba or
Costa Rica of the sweet flesh, and
a wooden shack in one of the mosquito marshes
in Manahawkin or the Outer Banks.
I am planning my cup of tea
and my sweet biscuit,
or my macaroni soup
and my can of sardines.
If I spent the morning washing shirts
I would read for two hours
before I slept through the afternoon.
If I walked first, or swam,
I might feel like writing down words
before I went in for coffee, or more hot water.
I will sit on the black rocks
to make my connections,
near the small basin of foam.
I will look at the footprints

going in and out of the water
and dream up a small blue god to talk to.
I will be just where I was
twenty-five years ago,
breathing in salt,
snorting like a prophet,
turning over the charred wood;
just where I was then,
getting rid of baggage,
living in dreams,
finding a way to change, or sweeten, my clumsy life.

IV | PARADISE POEMS

1984

THE DANCING

In all these rotten shops, in all this broken furniture
and wrinkled ties and baseball trophies and coffee pots
I have never seen a post-war Philco
with the automatic eye
nor heard Ravel's "Bolero" the way I did
in 1945 in that tiny living room
on Beechwood Boulevard, nor danced as I did
then, my knives all flashing, my hair all streaming,
my mother red with laughter, my father cupping
his left hand under his armpit, doing the dance
of old Ukraine, the sound of his skin half drum,
half fart, the world at last a meadow,
the three of us whirling and singing, the three of us
screaming and falling, as if we were dying,
as if we could never stop—in 1945—
in Pittsburgh, beautiful filthy Pittsburgh, home
of the evil Mellons, 5,000 miles away
from the other dancing—in Poland and Germany—
of God of mercy, oh wild God.

ORANGE ROSES

I am letting two old roses stand for everything I believe in.
I am restricting the size of the world, keeping it inside that plastic pot.
This is like Greece, the roses sitting in the hot sun,
the leaves exhausted,
the blue sky surrounding them.

I reach my fingers inside the dirt
and slowly scrape the sides.
One more flower will bloom the rest of this month,
probably symbolizing the last breath left
after a lifetime of tearful singing.

The wall in back of me is no part of this.
It shows only a large shadow overcome with thought.
It shows him in ruins,
his body spread out in all directions,
his pencil uprooted, his own orange roses dark and hidden.

PICKING THE ROSES

I am picking the roses for next time,
Little Darlings for the side of the house,
Tiffany and Lilli Marlene for the hot slope
where the strawberries used to be.
I am doing this in early February
before the ice cracks and the island gets back its dignity.
There is a towel against the front door
to keep the wind out
and newspapers squeezed into the holes
so we can have good reading for the bright wasps.
If there is a boar, he is outside snorting.
We will need him for the bleeding and regeneration to come.

Soon the dead plants will arrive by mail,
the roses in corrugated paper, their roots packed
in excelsior and moss,
the lilies in plastic bags, *their* roots like radishes,
a leaf or two to signify the good life of the future.
When the time comes I will walk outside to hear my name
ring through the trees, or stop for a minute to hear the words skip
on the water or collect like mice behind the garbage cans.
I will tear the ground with my shovel
and bark with pain as I bend down over the roots
and get ready for the dirty water and the dust.

Then for two blocks up and two blocks down
my screams, and the screams of the boar,
will mix together.
There will be talking afterwards and sobbing
and touches of cynicism and histrionics
in the living rooms by the river,
and single voices wailing in the tradition
of the old Orient, and choruses of flies
boring everybody with their small details,
crash of bone against bone,
mixture of broken weapons and falling shadows.

I will clean up
like a ghost at my own funeral.
My poor left eye will be closed shut

behind its puffy hill
and my right thigh will be permanently twisted.
I will sleep my sleep
on top of the mohair sofa,
over the *Inquirer* and the white espresso.
In one month
the twigs will be shining
and I will be rocking in my metal chair
or sitting on my swing
in the little room on the side porch.
One arm I'll hold up in the snake position
above my head
and one arm I'll hold out like a hairy fox
waiting to spring.
I will collect all the stupidity and sorrow
of the universe in one place
and wait—like everyone else—
for the first good signs,
the stems to turn green,
the buds to swell and redden,
the clouds to fall, the trees to bend,
the tenors of all 3,000 counties
to tremble in the grass,
to beat their chests, to tear their shirts,
to stumble against the sopranos, to rise and fall
like birds in the muddy grass,
like heavy birds in last year's muddy grass.

IN MEMORY OF W. H. AUDEN

I am going over my early rages again,
my first laments and ecstasies,
my old indictments and spiritualities.
I am standing, like Schiller, in front of Auden's door
waiting for his carved face to let me in.
In my hand is *The Poem of My Heart* I dragged
from one ruined continent to the other,
all my feelings slipping out on the sidewalk.
It was warm and hopeful in his small cave
waiting for the right word to descend
but it was cold and brutal outside on Fourth Street
as I walked back to the Seventh Avenue subway,
knowing, as I reached the crowded stairway,
that I would have to wait for ten more years
or maybe twenty more years for the first riches
to come my way, and knowing that the stick
of that old Prospero would never rest
on my poor head, dear as he was with his robes
and his books of magic, good and wise as he was
in his wrinkled suit and his battered slippers.
—Oh good and wise, but not enough to comfort me,
so loving was he with his other souls.
I had to wait like clumsy Caliban,
a sucker for every vagueness and degeneration.
I had to find my own way back, I had to
free myself, I had to find my own pleasure
in my own sweet cave, with my own sweet music.
    Once a year, later even once a month,
I stood on the shores of Bleecker and Horatio
waving goodbye to that ship all tight and yare
and that great wizard, bobbing up and down
like a dreaming sailor out there, disappearing
just as he came, only this time his face more weary
and his spirit more grave than when he first arrived
to take us prisoner on our own small island,
that poet I now could talk to, that wrinkled priest
whose neck I'd hang on, that magician
who could release me now, whom I release and remember.

ROMANIA, ROMANIA

I stand like some country crow across the street
from the Romanian Synagogue on Rivington Street
singing songs about Moldavia and Bukovina.
I am a walking violin, screeching
a little at the heights, vibrating a little
at the depths, plucking sadly on my rubber guts.
It's only music that saves me. Otherwise
I would be keeping the skulls forever, otherwise
I would be pulling red feathers from my bloody neck.
It's only music, otherwise I would be white
with anger or giving in to hatred
or turning back to logic and religion—
the Brahms Concerto, hills and valleys of gold,
the mighty Kreutzer, rubies piled over rubies,
a little Bartók, a little ancient Bach—
but more for the thin white tablecloths under the trees
than for Goga and his Christians,
and more for the red petticoats and the cold wine and the garlic
than the railroad station and the submachine guns,
and more for the little turn on Orchard Street
and the life of sweetness and more for the godly Spanish
and the godly Chinese lined up for morning prayers,
and much much more for the leather jackets on sticks
and the quiet smoke
and the plush fire escapes,
and much much more for the silk scarves in the windows
and the cars in the streets
and the dirty invisible stars—
Yehudi Menuhin
wandering through the hemlocks,
Jascha Heifetz
bending down over the tables,
the great Stern himself
dragging his heart from one ruined soul to another.

IT'S NICE TO THINK OF TEARS

It's nice to think of tears as polliwogs
rolling down your face,
lost on the cheekbones and the distant chin
before they drop on the oilcloth and the pine floor.

It's nice to think of you reaching your hand up
and wiping them away,
all that sadness
welling up, then disappearing.

It's just fantastic to think of sorrow
as water,
to think of it dripping through the leaves
or escaping in the sand,

to see it stretching from one salt island
to another,
or filling the cellar up
and the pools and ditches—

all that grief
where the eyes were,
all that sobbing
where the heart was,

all those rivers flowing
where the swelling had been,
and all those lakes and oceans
where the head was lying,

where the mouth was open,
where the shoulders were bent,
where the hands were hanging down,
where the dark old hands were helpless and hanging down.

SONG

There's nothing in this gardenous world more delightful
than blossoms lying where they fall,
soldiers sprawled from one ravine to another,
lovers under a bloody window.

I look up through the branches
dreaming of fate.
My old enemy the blue sky is above me.
My old enemy the hawk
is moving slowly through the string of white clouds.

One day I will wake up at dawn
and philosophize about my state
as I get ready.
I will put on my heavy shirt
and think of the long and bitter day ahead.

It will take hours to know
whether I will live or die,
which car to get ready,
which woods to pass by,
which animal to ride over,
which bridge to cross on the way.

I love the sight of me
rolled over on the ground.
I love being pierced through the heart,
half a man, half a flower,
reaching my hand out, turning my palm away,
one of the many pink and white blossoms,
one of the many on the brutal lawn.

WEEPING AND WAILING

I like the way my little harp makes trees
leap, how putting the metal between my teeth
makes half the animals in my backyard quiver,
how plucking the sweet tongue makes the stars
live together in love and ecstasy.

I bend my face and cock my head. My eyes
are open wide listening to the sound.
My hand goes up and down like a hummingbird.
My mouth is opening and closing, I am singing
in harmony, I am weeping and wailing.

HIDDEN JUSTICE

This is my forest now, this Christmas cactus,
stretching out leaf after leaf,
pink blossom after pink blossom.
This is where I'll go to breathe
and live in darkness
and sit like a frog, and sit like a salamander,
and this is where I'll find a tiny light
and have my vision
and start my school—
in this dry and airy place
beside these trunks
in this fragrant mixture.

I will put my small stage here
under a thick leaf
and I will eat and sleep and preach right here
and put my two dogs there
to keep my two guards busy
with prayer and feeding.
I will live completely for the flowering,
my neck like a swan's,
my fingers clawing the air
looking for justice;
year after year the same,
my fingers clawing the air for hidden justice.

CHRISTMAS STICKS

Before I leave I'll put two sticks on the porch
so they can talk to each other about poor Poland
and wrap themselves around each other the way sticks
do when most of life is gone. They will lie
a little about Walesa, one will dance
and shake his dried-out leaves as if to threaten
the other, one will lean against the wall
as if there were boots to give him courage, as if
there was a moustache somewhere there among the scars
and a thin sword and a thin tear. I'd make them flower
again, I'd make them drive through Warsaw
on the back of trucks, I'd have them reach their wooden
hands through the flimsy slats and take the gifts
and live out the dream of 1830 and the dream
of 1863, the Russians gone,
the Germans gone, the life remade, the flags
flying over the factories, workers dancing
above the trees, a wedding under a walnut,
the food amazing, the last memory the bride's
father in white showing his empty pockets,
his beard a little white to match his suit,
his eyes all wet, his shirt half open—
all that sweetness, all that golden fat—
the fat I love, the sweetness I love—and the two of them
walking home at night after the wedding
talking to each other again about Pulaski
and Casimir the Great and Copernicus
and what it could have been if only sticks
had ruled the vicious world, remembering again
the Jews arriving from Spain, the scholars of Europe
descending on Cracow, half the Italian painters
living in Poland, the gentry reading books,
the women drawing and playing flutes—
forgetting the dream-crushers out there in the swamps,
forgetting the liars, forgetting the murderers—
two sticks in the moonlight carrying on
after the wedding, lifting their empty bottles
for the last time, one of them heaving his over
a sycamore—a buttonwood tree—one of them
heaving his across a frozen river

and listening with his hands on his bent knees
for the old crash, slow in coming, the impact
a half a minute later than he expected,
both of them laughing at the stupidity,
both of them weeping for the huge carp
frozen in mud, and both of them toasting the bride
with broken hands, with nothing this time, with fingers
ruined and shredded, kissing the dear one goodbye
before they go off like wounded soldiers, home
from fighting the Turks at Vienna, home from fighting
the Deutschers a hundred times and the Rooskies two hundred,
home from fighting the Swedes and the Austrians,
two great masters of suffering and sadness
singing songs about love and regeneration.

THE SAME MOON ABOVE US

When I see a man sleeping over the grilles
trying to get some heat for his poor stomach
then I think he must be Ovid dreaming
again of Rome, getting ready to write
another letter to Caesar, his third that day,
his tenth or eleventh that week, keeping track
somewhere in those dirty sweaters and coats
of what they owe him now that his labor is over,
now that he's lying there with his hands all grimy
and his face all ruined—

Although I think he is sometimes caught by the horror
as if he had just come to, as if he could finally
let the bitterness take over and just sit there
with his coats wrapped around him, his stinking animal skins
dragging through ice and mud, his mind and body
finally alike, the pedant's dream come true,
the mystic's dream, the lover's dream, his brain
reduced to pulp, his heart surrounded,
his only desire a little warmth, a fire
for his poor fingers, a fire for his poor toes—

I think in his fifties he learned a new language
to go with the freezing rain; he would have done this
anyhow, he would have shouldered his riches
and stripped things down the way men in their fifties
do, only this way he found it easy,
he only had to lift his cold face
from his thin notebook, he only had to look
at the street full of garbage and there he was.
He did have to find another instrument
since flutes wouldn't do and reeds wouldn't do
and the rattle of pencils on the metal grates
wouldn't do—

I see him lying there watching the wind cleaning
the blue sky, pulling a piece of sock
over his raw ankle, asking himself
what he was punished for. Was it because
he sang too much? Was it because

he was too playful, too pathetic? No one could possibly
know him here in New York City outside
the Prince Hotel and the twenty-eight marble steps;
no one could see him with his paper cup
staring up at the dirty ceiling,
trying to remember Love's reception, the white
horses waiting for him, the golden plates
with purple dolphins on them, all that happiness
the one time in his life—

What he thinks he can do sometimes is find
a way to live in this world without rotting
from too much thought, and he thinks he can sometimes walk
past the galvanized soil pipe or the Sid Vicious sign
or even sit all night in his plastic chair
across from the amazing brass ash tray
without half dying; and he thinks he can be an eagle again
and talk to Caesar, and he thinks sometimes, if he's lucky,
he can have his muse back and eat
from her sweet fingers just as he did before
and listen to her song against his lips
as if he were holding the sea in his black hands,
as if, after first giving him all that power,
she now could give him pity and consolation,
now that he's living in horror,
now that his hair is white and his feet are frozen,
she who lives on the side of Helicon,
the muse of luscious sight and lovely sorrow,
he who lives at Third and Houston,
the genius of murdered love—

Although he knows that without this last voyage
he would be only another ruined poet,
and this is his glory—Prince Street is his glory.
The truth is he has become his own sad poem,
he walks and eats and sleeps in total sadness,
sadness is even what he calls his life, he
is the teacher of sadness, there are no limits
to his bitter song, he sits at the long bar
across the street from New York Kitchen
drinking sadness—mixed with wine—
and it is his own regret that moves him to tears
and his own sorrow that saves him—he is saved
by his own sorrow—it is his victory—

And it is his victory that though he lay
bored and oppressed for the last ten years
he sang like no one else before him did
about himself and his own suffering.
He was the first, and since he wrote
in innocence both the remorse and pity
are almost forgivable. It is hard to think
of Coleridge without an Ovid first or Pound
alive in the cage without him. I myself
feel almost happy that he came before me,
that my own wailing
found such a model in his books of sorrow.
In my lighter moments when my cheeks
are dry and my heart is not yet pounding
I like to compare his heaviness to mine—
or mine to his—to see whose chair is older,
whose rug is thinner, whose hands are colder,
although the world I live and wander in
is really not like his, at least not yet—

And when the color south of Cooper Union
settles into mauve or streaky violet
I leave him lecturing his loyal wife
or cursing his rotten enemies
and make my way to the broken-down subway stop
at Spring and Broadway, humming in both languages,
the white moon above me, the dirt somewhere beneath me,
the sidewalks crazy again, the lights in Jersey,
the lights in Manhattan, like the fires in Rome,
burning again without me, I on the edge
of Empire walking west in the snow, my neck
now raw, my feet now raw, my eyes gone blind,
the last one on the streets, the last poet left
who lives like this, the last one who does a dance
because of the dirty ice and the leather boots,
alone in the middle of nowhere, no one to see
his gorgeous retrieval, no one to shake the air
with loud applause and no one to turn and bow to
in the middle of his exile ten cold minutes
before he leaves the street for his soft pillow
and his other exile, far from Rome's domain,
and far from New York's domain, now silent and peaceful.

LEAVING ANOTHER KINGDOM

FOR PHIL LEVINE

I think this year I'll wait for the white lilacs
before I get too sad.
I'll let the daffodils go, flower by flower,
and the blue squill, and the primroses.
Levine will be here by then,
waving fountain pens, carrying rolled-up posters
of Ike Williams and King Levinsky.
He will be reaching into his breast pocket
for maps of grim Toledo
showing the downtown grilles and the bus stations.
He and I together
will get on our hands and knees
on the warm ground
in the muddy roses
under the thorn tree.
We will walk the mile to my graveyard
without one word of regret,
two rich poets
going over the past a little,
changing a thing or two,
making a few connections,
doing it all with balance,
stopping along the way to pet a wolf,
slowing down at the locks,
giving each other lectures on early technology,
mentioning eels and snakes,
touching a little on our two cities,
cursing our Henrys a little,
his Ford, my Frick,
being almost human about it, almost decent,
sliding over the stones to reach the island,
throwing spears on the way,
staring for twenty minutes at two robins
starting a life together in rural Pennsylvania,
kicking a heavy tire, square and monstrous,
huge and soggy, maybe a '49 Hudson,
maybe a '40 Packard, maybe a Buick
with mohair seats and silken cords
and tiny panes of glass—both of us seeing

the same car, each of us driving
our own brick road, both of us whistling
the same idiotic songs, the tops of trees flying,
houses sailing along, the way they did then,
both of us walking down to the end of the island
so we could put our feet in the water, so I could
show him where the current starts, so we could
look for bottles and worn-out rubbers, Trojans
full of holes, the guarantee run out—
love gone slack and love gone flat—
a few feet away from New Jersey near the stones
that look like large white turtles guarding the entrance
to the dangerous channel where those lovers—Tristan
and his Isolt, Troilus and you know who,
came roaring by on inner tubes, their faces
wet with happiness, the shrieks and sighs
left up the river somewhere, now their fingers
trailing through the wake, now their arms out
to keep themselves from falling, now in the slow part
past the turtles and into the bend, we sitting there
putting on our shoes, he with Nikes,
me with Georgia loggers, standing up
and smelling the river, walking single file
until we reach the pebbles, singing in French
all the way back, losing the robins forever,
losing the Buick, walking into the water,
leaving another island, leaving another
retreat, leaving another kingdom.

FOR SONG

I am sitting thirty feet above the water
with my hand at my throat,
listening to the owls go through the maples
and the seaplanes go up and down like cracked buzz saws.

I am finding my own place
in the scheme of things
between the nation of Reuben half drunk on twisted coneflowers
and the nation of Dan all crazy for weird veronica.

I am paying attention to providence,
the silver hordes this time,
the mud up to my knees,
the glass on my fingers.

I am studying paradise and the hereafter,
a life beyond compare,
a great log thrown up for my own pleasure,
an unbelievably large and cold and beneficent sun.

I am lifting a blade of grass to my wet lips
for music;
I am trying a dozen fruits and flowers
to get one sound;

I am twisting my head around, I am slowly clapping
for harmony;
I am raising my eyes, I am listening to the worms
for song.

MY SWALLOWS

For hours I sit here facing the white wall
and the dirty swallows. If I move too much,
I will lose everything, if I even breathe,
I'll lose the round chest and the forked tail
and the nest above the window, under the ceiling.

As far as shame, I think I have lived too long
with only the moonlight coming in to worry
too much about what it looks like. I have given
a part of my mind away, for what it's worth
I have traded half of what I have—

I'll call it half—so I can see these smudges
in the right light. I think I live in ruins
like no one else, I see myself as endlessly
staring at what I lost, I see me mourning
for hours, either worn away with grief

or touched with simple regret, but free this time
to give myself up to loss alone. I mourn
for the clumsy nest and I mourn for the two small birds
sitting up there above the curtains watching—
as long as I am there—and I mourn for the sky

that makes it clear and I mourn for my two eyes
that drag me over, that make me sit there singing,
or mumbling or murmuring, at the cost
of almost everything else, my two green eyes,
my brown—my hazel, flecked with green and brown—

and this is what I'll do for twenty more years,
if I am lucky—even if I'm not—I'll live
with the swallows and dip through the white shadows
and rest on the eaves and sail above the window.
This is the way I *have* lived, making a life

for more than twenty years—for more than forty—
out of this darkness; it was almost a joy,
almost a pleasure, not to be foolish or maudlin,
sitting against my wall, closing my eyes,
singing my dirges.

BERKELEY

Today I saw the weird leg of Apollo
go in after Daphne—it was either cyprus
or Monterey pine, I am so blind and ignorant
of West Coast flora. I saw the wood waver
and the ground shake; I sat on my black briefcase
looking up at the leaves. I who am so
wondrous, I who always looked for Messiahs,
I who gave opinions, caught up now
in a new strangeness thousands of miles away
from my own cold river, learning quickly to eat
the other foods, learning to love
the way they do, walking after them
with my mouth half open, starting gently to teach,
doing the wind first, doing the dark old days
before there was even wind, saving Picasso
for Monday or Tuesday, saving the two dark strings
for Wednesday night, the night of the dozen tears,
saving New York
for the trip back to the airport, pushing the door
with tapered fingers, racing down the belt
with all that fire around me, sitting by the window
with only three minutes to go. Swinging my briefcase
with all the secrets inside. Keeping my secrets.
Thinking of Poland again. Getting ready for snow.

BEE BALM

Today I'm sticking a shovel in the ground
and digging up the little green patch
between the hosta and the fringe bleeding heart.
I am going to plant bee balm there
and a few little pansies till the roots take
and the leaves spread out in both directions.

This is so the hummingbird will rage
outside my fireplace window; this is so
I can watch him standing in the sun
and hold him a little above my straining back,
so I can reach my own face up to his
and let him drink the sugar from my lips.

This is so I can lie down on the couch
beside the sea horse and the glass elephant,
so I can touch the cold wall above me
and let the yellow light go through me,
so I can last the rest of the summer on thought,
so I can live by secrecy and sorrow.

VIVALDI YEARS

I lay forever, didn't I, behind those old windows,
listening to Bach and resurrecting my life.
I slept sometimes for thirty or forty minutes
while the violins shrieked and the cellos trembled.
It was a crazy youth, wasn't it, letting
my mind soar like that, giving myself
up to poetry the way I did.
It was a little like Goethe's, wasn't it,
a little like Eugene O'Neill's, one joyous
sadness after another. That was the everlasting
life, wasn't it. The true world without end.

MOSCOW

for Diane Freund

I love to bend down over my love,
my crayon at her breast, my lips just over her neck.
I love her eyes following my left hand,
her fingers rubbing the Greek blanket.
I love the sunlight on the cold windows,
the horns of Scriabin rising through the dreary street,
the carved houses forever on our wild faces.

TODAY A LEAF

FOR WILLIAM MERWIN

Today it was just a dry leaf that told me
I should live for love.
It wasn't the six birds sitting like little angels
in the white birch tree,
or the knife I use to carve my pear with.
It was a leaf, that had read Tolstoi, and Krishnamurti,
that had loved William James,
and put sweet Jesus under him where he could be safe forever.
"The world is so bright," he said. "You should see the light."
"We are born without defenses, both babies and leaves."
"The branch is necessary, but it is in the way."
"I am not afraid. I am never afraid."
Then he stretched his imaginary body
this way and that.
He weighs a half a gram, is brown and green,
with two large mold spots on one side, and a stem
that curls away, as if with a little pride,
and he could be easily swept up and forgotten,
but oh he taught me love for two good hours,
and helped me with starvation, and dread, and dancing.
As far as I'm concerned his grave is here
beside me,
next to the telephone and the cupful of yellow pencils,
under the window, in the rich and lovely presence
of Franz Joseph Haydn and Domenico Scarlatti and Gustav Mahler
forever.

SINGING

I have been waiting for a month
for this squirrel to dissolve in water.
I couldn't afford the disgrace
of dumping it onto the ground
and watching its body lurch and its teeth chatter.

There is such ghoulishness now
that it might drag its back legs after it,
such desperation
that I might rub its shoulders or brush its lips
to bring it back to life.

You who rushed home to masturbate,
you who touched the same red flower every day,
you know how I must skirt this lawn
to avoid the barrel.
You know how I live in silence.

You who knelt on the frozen leaves,
you know how dark it got under the ice;
you know how hard it was to live
with hatred, how long it took to convert
death and sadness into beautiful singing.

AT JANE'S

FOR GIL ORLOVITZ, 1919–1974

I touch the rose to see what happens there
before I go inside to eat, I pull
the clothesline down and kick the cracked cement,
I howl to myself for mercy. One more time
I walk through the rotten tomatoes. I will end
with little leaves on my shoes, with spoonfuls of mud,
with a beating heart, with a mouth that's open—
I hold my arm out straight like a dirty drunk,
I walk the plank between the rhododendron
and the little pear. For all I know
I could live here happy, I could walk
from here to the river and back without a thought.
I could stop at the Super-America
and read the morning paper. I could sit
at my pancake dreaming of heaven, smiling like a lamb,
listening vaguely to all the garbage, finding
my cave and my twine, my dark place, chewing and listening
while inside I wander—I beg for justice—I crawl
through hell for a little justice. I turn to the wall
and sing a little, and dance a little—
just as the fall is breaking on the Ohio,
the leaves are turning yellow, in Marietta,
the backyards stretching out for hundreds of yards
the way they do in America, all that richness,
all that Utopia, wasted, a little dog
howling out there, inside we're barking, inside
I'm finding another heaven, I'm turning around
this way and that, I'm finding my hole in the sun . . .
We're talking now about Spanish music, the difference
in soul between northern Europe and southern Europe;
we're talking now about Crete, we're talking
about Robert Lowell and Delmore Schwartz; I'm lecturing
on Orlovitz, I'm talking about his sonnets,
I'm talking about his death on West End Avenue,
about the poet we lost, about his life,
about the dull politics of poesy,
about the nineteenth century, about Keats,
eighty miles from Wheeling, West Virginia,
a million miles from Rome. Poor Orlovitz,
he wrote 500 poems. I remember the letters:

"Is this a poem, could you send me twenty bucks?"
What do I do with him now? He fell in the street
in front of a doorman; oh his death was superb,
the doorman blew his whistle, Orlovitz climbed
into a yellow cab, he'd never disappoint
a doorman. Now I'm brooding a little, absent,
the way I get, listening to the refrigerator,
the only music we have in North America,
cursing the Reagans a little, saying inside
one of Orlovitz's poems, going back again
into the cave, remembering Shelley's words
about his cave, and Vergil's, and Milton's, knowing
that mine is like theirs, a half mile underground,
where you go on your knees, where you keep the candle outside—
the underground journey—shivers and tremblings. We walk
to the river after breakfast, I'm in heaven,
I saw the meadow, I heard the voices, I felt
the light on my face—in Marietta, Ohio—
with Rachael Stern and Jack Killian and Jane
Somerville, there are alleys between the yards,
it is the oldest city in Ohio,
I wore my black suit for the reading, I roared
and whispered through forty poems, I sat like a lamb
in the mayor's living room, I sat like a dove
eating cheese and smiling, talking and smiling,
thinking my thoughts, my wise and tender thoughts,
the mayor's palace, Marietta, Ohio.

JOHN'S MYSTERIES

I've been seeing these tombstone beef sticks
and that umbrella tree in so many cities
that I forget where it is I am,
whether it's dirty John's I'm standing in line in
with onions and T-bone steaks in my hands,
or Bishop's, I think it was Bishop's, with hard salami,
safflower mayonnaise and two-percent milk.
My own system of perfect retrieval
tells me it's a big-leaved catalpa,
not an umbrella tree, and what it grows
is not cigars, but intricate seed stalks, terrible
to smoke, cancerless, tasteless, drooping and beautiful.
But I believe only in the islands
so I will insist on emptying the parking lot
of the two beer trucks and putting a table there
under the cigar tree, for me and my friends to eat at.
We will take three hours and end by turning
on the lights and leaning back in exhaustion.
We will be so happy about where we are
that we will cry for sadness, cursing everything
and anything from changed emotional conditions
to polluted leaves to emigration laws
that could threaten to end our mysteries and pleasures.
We will keep the napkins as souvenirs
and write, in ink, what it was like to live here
on Gilbert Street and Market, on Sixth and Pine,
in a town in Crete eight miles from Omalos,
a mile or so from the crone and her great-granddaughter
selling warm Coca-Colas on the flat
at the end of the deepest gorge in Europe—
if Crete is in Europe—at a lovely table with lights
hanging from the trees, a German there to remind us
of the Parachute Corps in 1941,
a Turk for horror, a Swede for humor, an Israeli
to lecture us, the rest of us from New Jersey
and California and Michigan and Georgia,
eating the lamb and drinking the wine, adoring it,
as if we were still living on that sea,
as if in Crete there had not been a blossom,
as if it had not fallen in Greece and Italy,

some terrible puzzle in great Knossos
Sir Arthur Evans is still unravelling,
the horrors spread out in little pieces
as if it were a lawn sale or foreclosure.
—I like to think of it that way, him on the grass there
putting together our future, the seven of us,
the eight of us, by the sea—looking at Libya—
this way, looking that way, this way, that way,
watching him with curiosity and terror,
wondering if he'll get it right, wondering how much
it's really in his hands, wanting a little
to tamper with it, getting a little irritated
with so much of it lying on the ground,
wanting it to be as it once was,
wanting the bull to bellow,
wanting him to snort and shake the ground,
wanting it to be luminous again,
Daedalus and Minos, Pasiphaë squealing with love,
the dear Parisian with her breasts exposed,
little courtyards where we could see the light,
little airways and passageways, pretty steps
going up and down, those parapets where friends
could look at the waves and talk about their sorrows,
those giant jars where all our wines and oils
were stored, those paintings that made us remember, those flutes
that made us dance, that put a lilt in our walk—
Our lives are in his hands, he goes through his wallet
to see if he has money to pay the bearers;
he touches his chest to see if he will die
before his work is done, he puts his camera
in front of the sun, he finds another fragment
that tells him something, he is cradling his elbow,
he is touching his chin, to help him think—
Sir Arthur Evans, angel of death—I walk
up Gilbert Street to reach my house. I live
with music now, and dance, I lie alone
waiting for sweetness and light. I'm balanced forever
between two worlds, I love what we had, I love
dreaming like this, I'm finding myself in the charts
between the white goat and the black, between
the trade with Sicily and the second palace, between
the wave of the sea and the wave of the sky, I am
a drop of white paint, I am the prow of a ship,
I am the timbers, I am the earthquake—
in eighty or ninety years

someone will dream of Crete again and see me
sitting under this tree and study me
along with the baskets and the red vases.
I'll walk across here touching one beer truck
with my left hand and one with my other.
I'll put my old stone arms around his neck
and kiss him on the lip and cheek, I'll sing
again and again
until he remembers me, until he remembers
the green catalpa pushing through the cement
and the little sticks of meat inside, his own
wild voyage behind him, his own sad life ahead.

SOAP

Here is a green Jew
with thin black lips.
I stole him from the men's room
of the Amelia Earhart and wrapped him in toilet paper.
Up the street in *Parfumes*
are Austrian Jews and Hungarian,
without memories really,
holding their noses in the midst of that
paradise of theirs.
There is a woman outside
who hesitates because it is almost Christmas.
"I think I'll go in and buy a Jew," she says.
"I mean some soap, some nice new lilac or lily
to soothe me over the hard parts,
some Zest, some Fleur de Loo, some Wild Gardenia."

And here is a blue Jew.
It is his color, you know,
and he feels better buried in it, imprisoned
in all that sky, the land of death and plenty.
If he is an old one he dances,
or he sits stiffly,
listening to the meek words and admiring the vile actions
of first the Goths and then the Ostrogoths.
Inside is a lovely young girl,
a Dane, who gave good comfort
and sad support to soap of all kinds and sorts
during the war and during the occupation.
She touches my hand with unguents and salves.
She puts one under my nose all wrapped in tissue,
and squeezes his cheeks.

I buy a black Rumanian for my shelf.
I use him for hair and beard,
and even for teeth when things get bitter and sad.
He had one dream, this piece of soap,
if I'm getting it right,
he wanted to live in Wien
and sit behind a hedge on Sunday afternoon
listening to music and eating a tender schnitzel.

That was delirium. Other than that he'd dream
of America sometimes, but he was a kind of cynic,
and kind of lazy—conservative—even in his dream,
and for this he would pay, he paid for his lack of dream.
The Germans killed him because he didn't dream
enough, because he had no vision.

I buy a brush for my back, a simple plastic
handle with gentle bristles. I buy some dust
to sweeten my body. I buy a yellow cream
for my hairy face. From time to time I meet
a piece of soap on Broadway, a sliver really,
without much on him, sometimes I meet two friends
stuck together the way those slivers get
and bow a little, I bow to hide my horror,
my grief, sometimes the soap is so thin
the light goes through it, these are the thin old men
and thin old women the light goes through, these are
the Jews who were born in 1865
or 1870, for them I cringe, for them
I whimper a little, they are the ones who remember
the eighteenth century, they are the ones who listened
to heavenly voices, they were lied to and cheated.

My counterpart was born in 1925
in a city in Poland—I don't like to see him born
in a little village fifty miles from Kiev
and have to fight so wildly just for access
to books, I don't want to see him struggle
half his life to see a painting or just to
sit in one of the plush chairs listening to music.
He was dragged away in 1940
and turned to some use in 1941,
although he may have fought a little, piled
some bricks up or poured some dirty gasoline
over a German truck. His color was rose
and he floated for me for days and days; I love
the way he smelled the air, I love how he looked,
how his eyes lighted up, how his cheeks were almost pink
when he was happy. I loved how he dreamed, how he almost
disappeared when he was in thought. For him
I write this poem, for my little brother, if I
should call him that—maybe he is the ghost
that lives in the place I have forgotten, that dear one
that died instead of me—oh ghost, forgive me!—

Maybe he stayed so I could leave, the *older* one
who stayed so I could leave—oh live forever!
forever!—Maybe he is a Being from the other
world, his left arm agate, his left eye crystal,
and he has come back again for the twentieth time,
this time to Poland, to Warsaw or Bialystok,
to see what hell is like. I think it's that,
he has come back to live in our hell, if he could
even prick his agate arm or even weep
with those crystal eyes—oh weep with your crystal eyes,
dear helpless Being, dear helpless Being. I'm writing this
in Iowa and Pennsylvania and New York City,
in time for Christmas, 1982,
the odor of Irish Spring, the stench of Ivory.

I PITY THE WIND

I am taking off my glasses
so I can stare at the little candles
and the glass of water
in pure darkness.

I am letting a broom stand
for my speech on justice
and an old thin handkerchief
for the veil of melodrama I have worn for thirty years.

I am dragging in Euripides
for his strange prayer
and my own true Hosea
for his poem on love and loyalty.

After a minute I fall down dead
from too much thought
and turn to the freezing wall
for an hour of quiet sadness.

I start my practice later,
twenty minutes for breathing,
twenty minutes for song,
twenty minutes for liberation and ritual.

My poem is about the airshaft
and Zoroaster
and the soul caught in its last struggle
with the two-headed cow, father of everything.

My elation has something to do with light,
my misery with darkness,
my secrecy and fear and distance
with neither.

I end up with a pillow
and a painted floor, as I always do,
my head on the flowers, a little pocket for air,
my right arm drifting and dangling.

I end up just humming,
true to myself at last,
preparing myself for the bridge
and the hand that will lead me over, the hand I adore.

I pity this hero,
so in love with fire,
so warlike,
so bent on teaching.

Before the winter is over I'll have some sticks
for my dining room table and one or two large blooms
to take the place of the Norfolk pine
shredding and popping in the cold rain.

I'll pick some berries from the thin viburnum
and eat them as a bird does, one at a time,
jerking my head and looking around with terror,
studying the world with softened eyes.

I'll walk between the kitchen and the birch tree
a hundred times, a broom in one hand and either
a shovel or an ax in the other. I'll tie
a piece of frozen string around my finger

and either chew some bark or do a little
Esquimaux shuffling, and moaning, around the broken
circle of slate. I'll look for either a robin
or some other monster, maybe a yellow warbler

to go with my scarf. I'll count the days till Easter,
the thirteen Sundays, the Virgin Days, the Martyr Days,
the days of sleep and waking. Groundhog Day.
Valentine's Day. Ninety days in all.

The one or two cars that come by will be farting
their brains out trying to make it in the cold,
and no one will see me dying there in the twilight,
holding my hands up in the slippery branches.

I'll stay for ten more minutes before I go in,
enjoying the cold and letting the ice come into
my lungs and heart. Whatever my struggle is
I'll let it take place in this yard where the pile of stones

was, and the little hill—I'll keep it
between one tree and another, mostly away
from the flower bed and the wall, as close as I can
to the cement steps and the walk. I'll say goodnight

to one thing or another, maybe a headlight
from Route 611, maybe a brilliant oriole
come here to die in the dark. I'll drink my tea
and my Popov over the heater and with a knife

and screwdriver I'll scrape the snow from my boots.
I'll rest for six good hours and start my watch
again at six in the morning—who's to say
what happens in the night?—I'll look for a jay

to start me right, some pale-crested bluejay
lost and gone wild, some giant from the south
remembering his pine, some frightened animal
screaming for life, sliding on the branches,

wanting his meadow back. I'll pick him up,
though it's too late to put him inside my coat
against my chest, and it's too late to breathe
into his bony mouth. I'll wait for three

minutes, to do him justice, then I'll start
my icy walk—a part of the mystery—
and end up shaking my feathers from the cold,
a monster myself, with a piece of the loblolly

in my hip pocket, deciding, certainly before
Washington's Birthday, and certainly before Mother's Day,
whether it was worth it for our birds
to come so far for their wisdom, little simulacra

dying, as I do, from hunger and disease,
maybe two more to go today, the bastard
love and the bastard hope, maybe three,
the bastard pity, before I pull the blind up

and look at the moon, full and weeping tonight,
although it's past its prime and getting ready
for the last sliver again, then darkness again
and the first sliver again, ferocious phases.

ROMANCE

After thirty years
I am still listening to the pipes,
I am still enchanted
with the singing and moaning of the dry boards.

I am lying there night after night
thinking of water.
I am joining palms, or whistling Mozart
and early Yeats.

I am living without savagery,
stretching my body and turning on my left side
for music,
humming to myself and turning on my right side
for words.

THE NETTLE TREE

Mine was the nettle tree, the nettle tree.
It grew beside the garage and on the river
and I protected it from all destroyers.

I loved the hanging branches and the trunk
that grew like a pole. I loved the little crown
that waved like a feather. I sat for hours watching

the birds come in to eat the berries. I read
my Homer there—I wanted to stay forever
sleeping and dreaming. I put my head on the trunk

to hear my sounds. It was my connection for years,
half hanging in the wind—half leaning, half standing.
It was my only link. It was my luxury.

SYCAMORE

It was March third I came outside and saw
for the first time the buttonwood tree with last year's
leaves hanging in the wind like little hearts
and one or two crazy birds going mad with choices
in the hideous leftover snow and the slippery mud.
March the third. The branches were more a silver
than either green or tan, there was no fuzz
yet. Spring was still in Arizona, the Sonora
desert somewhere, somewhere in Ensenada,
and we were still gluing our frozen ears
to our crystal sets in Fairchild and Waterloo.
     The lower branches bend as if they were holding
castanets in their hands—this tree is Greek!—
maybe as if they were limp, the left hand is limp,
it is a tree from Greenwich Avenue,
from Fire Island, but the upper arms
reach out to plead for mercy, reach out to bless
us, she is a twenty-arm goddess, leaning
over a little, dancing her dance, making
little obscene gestures to the lord of lords,
a tiny finger here, a whole fist there.
     I open the windows, I pull the wooden strips
away from the sashes, I tear the dirty plastic,
I let the sun in. Soon my ties will be dancing,
soon my poems will be on the floor, I am
old Shivers, I do a turn to the left, to the right.
Where shall I go this year? What door will I open
and put a little primitive iron against?
Where shall I put the bucket? I want to live here
beside my tree and watch it change, the brown
give way to green, the green give way to brown.
I want, for once, to understand what happens
when the skin falls off. This tree is like a snake.
How many years does it live? What does it do
in its sleep? March thirty-first, this year,
is the little passage; we will get on our knees
and howl with freedom, not one of us can bear
to live without howling, we were given voices
so we could scream. I sing a song from Florida
about the life to come, someone is singing—

she is a flute, I am a silver harp—
about the seven openings, the soul
skittering, sacred things. I want her to go
so I can become a tree, so I can bury
myself as Daphne does, she is the one
who understands what it means to be tormented;
she calls the spring Apollo, Apollo tortured her,
he followed her from one bare tree to another.
I call it Apollo too, I take my place
inside the silver wood, at least for a year.
Next March the third I'll struggle out of my skin
like a sleepy girl, my hair will be too dry,
my nails too long, my mouth will start to work,
at first it will be too hoarse, and then too shrill;
I'll see the streets will be empty, there will be peace,
I'll walk to the graveyard and back, I'll walk to the lake,
no one will see me, no one will follow me
with rage in his eyes, with brutal love in his hands.
It is like death, isn't it, living in the tree,
listening to what were noises, feeling those changes
and knowing they weren't for you—I love the bells
when they come, I love standing in a grove
and guessing which one she's in—I'm in—if I were
Apollo I'd turn myself into this sycamore
and reach my arms through hers, I'd do some flashy
two-step that's made for heavy sycamores,
and when we lie it would be like two great animals,
sweat running down our faces, tears down our legs.
      This year when I sit at the table with bitter bread
in my hands I'll stop for one full minute to give
some lonely praise to the sycamore; I'll say,
let's stop a minute and think of the sycamore,
let's think of the lovely white branches, let's think of the bark,
let's think of the leaves, the three great maple lobes.
What does it know of liberation? I'll say.
What does it know of slavery, bending over
the streams of America? How does it serve as a text
for lives that are pinched, or terrified? Were there sycamores
along the banks of the Rhine or Oder? Tell me
about its bells again, those most of all,
the hard gray balls that dangle from the stems,
tell me about the bark, the large thin flakes,
and the colors, dark at the bottom, light at the top.
And I will go on for an hour storming and raving
before I drink my final cup of wine

and shout to the Egyptians—as I do every year—
you are my Apollo, you are my fleshpot, forgive me
for turning into a tree, forgive me, you lovers
of life for leaving you suddenly, how foolish
and cheated you must have felt, how foolish the body
must feel when it's only a carcass, when the breath
has left it forever, as it always does,
in search of something painless; and I'll end
by sprinkling the tree and sprinkling the ground around it
and holding my hand up for a second of silence,
since I am the one who runs the service—I am
the only one in this house, I do my reclining
all alone, I howl when I want, and I am,
should anyone come in, a crooked tree
leaning far out, I am a hundred feet tall,
I am a flowering figure, I am staggering
across the desert, and here I am now in New York
and here I am now in Pittsburgh, the perfect wilderness.

BAJA

These tiny Mexican mosquitoes are like lost souls
looking for blood among the white visitors
in their own land. They come to lead us through
some four or five old trees. They stoop to bite
our hands, they make that wailing sound I live
in terror of, they sing in our ears, they walk
between the seams, they reach for the drink they love,
they bend half over drinking,
they walk along the sand and through the flowers,
they look for work, they are looking for work, they pound
on the windows of our casita shouting *trabajo,*
trabajo, casting mournful eyes on the sea-wrack,
touching the broken sewer line and pointing
at the broken steps.   I catch one in a bottle
of Hellmann's and I let it loose outside
on the little plaza where the Citation is parked.
I tell him, my blood is for you, I tell him, remember
one Pennsylvanian who stopped to talk with the souls
and listened to them even if there was murder
and hatred between us; I ask about my future
as if I were Odysseus in hell
and he were Tiresias, that dear old lady,
or some other dead one, a Hercules or an Ajax.
He tells me, I think, to look out for my own
soul in the years to come, he tells me how long
it will be before I can rest a little, although
what he calls rest it may be some other thing
he talks about. He tells me there is a tree
and a yellow rock and a cloud. I should go left
around the tree, I should walk over the rock,
I should walk under the cloud; it is a Mexican
vision, full of darkness and secrecy.
I thank him for his kindness. Maybe he said
there is a room with terrible noises, tie
yourself to the kitchen table, hold your left hand
over your mouth, concentrate on living
a week at a time, divide your life into threes,
the terror can be digested, take care of yourself
when you are in New York, when you are sleeping,

when you are dying, there is a life to come—
or maybe he said, I love you more than anything,
have pity on me, please help me, take me with you,
I want the chance to live again, I can't
believe how large your limes were, oh I can't
believe how huge and clean your markets were;
take me with you, take me with you, wailing
and howling in front of me, in back of me,
pulling me down, the way they do, a swarm
of spirits, stumbling, pushing; I had to run,
I had to slam the door, I stood there freezing,
blood on the walls where I killed them, blood on my palms,
my forehead foolishly pounding, my two hands shaking,
all alone in the darkness, a man of the heart
making plans to the end, a screen for the terror,
a dish for the blood, a little love for strangers,
a little kindness for insects, a little pity for the dead.

KISSING STIEGLITZ GOOD-BYE

Every city in America is approached
through a work of art, usually a bridge
but sometimes a road that curves underneath
or drops down from the sky. Pittsburgh has a tunnel—

you don't know it—that takes you through the rivers
and under the burning hills. I went there to cry
in the woods or carry my heavy bicycle
through fire and flood. Some have little parks—

San Francisco has a park. Albuquerque
is beautiful from a distance; it is purple
at five in the evening. New York is Egyptian,
especially from the little rise on the hill

at 14-C; it has twelve entrances
like the body of Jesus, and Easton, where I lived,
has two small floating bridges in front of it
that brought me in and out. I said good-bye

to them both when I was 57. I'm reading
Joseph Wood Krutch again—the second time.
I love how he lived in the desert. I'm looking at the skull
of Georgia O'Keeffe. I'm kissing Stieglitz good-bye.

He was a city, Stieglitz was truly a city
in every sense of the word; he wore a library
across his chest; he had a church on his knees.
I'm kissing him good-bye; he was, for me,

the last true city; after him there were
only overpasses and shopping centers,
little enclaves here and there, a skyscraper
with nothing near it, maybe a meaningless turf

where whores couldn't even walk, where nobody sits,
where nobody either lies or runs; either that
or some pure desert: a lizard under a boojum,
a flower sucking the water out of a rock.

What is the life of sadness worth, the bookstores
lost, the drugstores buried, a man with a stick
turning the bricks up, numbering the shards,
dream twenty-one, dream twenty-two. I left

with a glass of tears, a little artistic vial.
I put it in my leather pockets next
to my flask of Scotch, my golden knife and my keys,
my joyful poems and my T-shirts. Stieglitz is there

beside his famous number; there is smoke
and fire above his head; some bowlegged painter
is whispering in his ear; some lady-in-waiting
is taking down his words. I'm kissing Stieglitz

good-bye, my arms are wrapped around him, his photos
are making me cry; we're walking down Fifth Avenue;
we're looking for a pencil; there is a girl
standing against the wall—I'm shaking now

when I think of her; there are two buildings, one
is in blackness, there is a dying poplar;
there is a light on the meadow; there is a man
on a sagging porch. I would have believed in everything.

ONE BIRD TO LOVE FOREVER

If I were to pick one bird to love forever
it would be the desert sparrow, sweetest
thing to ever live in Arizona,
sweetest thing of Mexico. I'd hold it
against my neck where the blood goes through, that soft
little nest underneath the chin, and stare at its eye
to hold it still, to keep it quiet. I'd let it
flutter, or let it fly, if it wanted. I'd rest
beside the acacia, beside the ironwood; I'd sit
for hours listening and loving.
                       When it flies
it rises like a junco, quick and crazy
to get away, and when it sits the softness of
birds is in its throat and chest. It has two
stripes, that is how we know it, one on the eye
and one extending down from the corner of the mouth
to make a pattern, white against the black,
and it has secret habits, it builds its nest
in some demented brush a hundred miles
from water—it never drinks, it seems to live
on nothing—I call it nothing but naturally
it thrives there. Joseph Wood Krutch, when he writes about the desert,
reminds us always that it is a paradise
for whatever lives there, the crazy trees, the lizards,
and nothing is deprived there, and nothing suffers,
it is their world, the funny quails and doves,
the sun shines on the needles, the spiders are huge,
the ground is always dry.
                  It is a madness
to think of loving that bird again. How could I
go back there anyhow? How would I live?
What would I do, go out to touch the thorns
and smell the flowers? Stand beside the boojum
and stare at the sky? Smile again like a lizard?
And Krutch is right—he's mostly right—the loving
of birds is useless, there is no true connection
between their lives and ours, they are only ideas.
It's always been that way, except when I read him—
I read him over and over—I see him using
his own bitterness as I have always used mine

to hide his weak heart behind, although the heart,
he'd say, is something like the liver, only coarser,
and he'd prefer the kidneys again for the seat
of all that soft emotion.
                              I only spent
five days in the desert but I'm going to drive
from Mexico to Salt Lake City next time.
My sparrow ranges from Texas to California
and north into Nevada and Idaho.
There is a photo in Cruikshank, she is perched
on the edge of her nest and four huge mouths are screaming
for food; the nest is almost buried between
the pads of a heavy cactus and the spines—
two inches, three inches long—surround the nest,
it looks like one or two go through the twisted
grass itself, but somehow they seem indifferent,
the delicate babies, the mother. I want to touch
the thorns and see how sharp the needles are.
I want to live there, I think, wake up with the sun
on my face, wake up with the light making a diamond
or hexagram on my chest and arms and glide
to the sink to drink my water, like a gecko.
My dream of dreams has me staring out the window,
my blue pants are held up by a rope,
and my elbows are leaning on a wooden washboard.
She looks at me for a second. She. A chittering
sparrow. Almost eating her way through the glass.
And then she moves to her tree, a hundred miles
away, for all I know, from my world, this silly
and rotten concrete shack, a poet's ugly
home away from home, a little flowerpot
holding the window up, a vague amazement
to her, a curiosity.
                          I look at the wind,
if you can look at the wind, and then I walk
for twenty or thirty minutes so I can find
my kidney on the road; I want to see it
weeping with pure self-pity, wringing its hands
the way a kidney wrings its hands, much better
than the liver, much better than the heart, more sadness
than either other organ. If I stand still,
if you catch me just right there is a cactus growing
out of my shoulder and my glasses are falling
as always; there is a look of wretched wisdom
on my red face—maybe there'll be a feather

with little bits of white on the outer edge
I'll put in my left pocket, maybe the stone
that goes with the feather, a tiny bit of pearl
to hold it down, you must hold feathers down,
and tiny bits of sand for the other pocket,
something to give me the desert again when I want it,
the blazing sunlight for grief, a little shade for the sorrow.

FRITZ

This is too good for words. I lie here naked
listening to Kreisler play. It is the touch
I love, that sweetness, that ease. I saw him once
at the end of the 40s, in Pittsburgh, I thought what he did
had something to do with his being old, his moving
to the front of the stage, his talking and smiling. I study
the cracks in the ceiling, the painted floors. I love him
because he strayed from the art, because he finished
his formal training at twelve, because he was whimsical
and full of secret humors. He is another one
I missed—I'm sick about it—there is no table
for us, no chairs to sit on, no words to remember.
He knew both Schönberg and Brahms, he visited
Dvořák, he studied theory with Bruckner,
he was a friend of Caruso's, he was a friend
of Pablo Casals.
                        Something like terror moves me,
walking on 611. What have we lost?
Does Kreisler belong to the dead? Was that a world
of rapture that he lived in? In what year
did he fix his imagination? Will there be strings
two hundred years from now? Will there be winds?
—There is a bank that leads down from the towpath
and I have walked there a thousand times, each time
half tripping over a certain root—I think
it is the root of a locust, maybe a lilac.
Tonight I am partly moody, partly in dread,
there is some pain in my neck, but I am still
possessed a little. I rush into the living room
to listen to either the Elgar or the Mendelssohn.
Something left us forever in 1912,
or 1914. Now we live off the rot.
I wonder if it's true. Kreisler was fifty
when he came back to Paris, over seventy
when I saw him in 1948. The root
was in the nineteenth century. I'm lost,
I'm lost without that century. There is
one movement left. *Con amore.* I began
my journey in 1947. I wrote
four hours a day, I read five books a week.

I had to read five books. I never knew
the right hand was raised like that. I never knew
how trapped the body was. I didn't believe
you gave yourself to the fire like that, that after
awhile—if the brain was in the fingers—the heart
was all that made the sound, whatever I mean
by "sound," and that we have to start with feeling—
we poor machines—which stood me in good stead
for ten or twenty years, that and Marlowe's
tears, and Coleridge's soft flight, and Dostoevski's
rack—it was the fire that moved me.

THREE SKIES

I always remember the crone. I always think of her
at that card table selling us Cokes. I sit in Dante's
drinking my coffee, my left hand is walking through Crete,
my right hand is lying exhausted on the roof
looking up at the stars. It was the stars
that helped me then. I stood on the cracked cement
on the same hill I know where Minos stood
looking for heavenly bulls and for the first time
in Greece I had my lightness. I saw the link
between that life and mine, I saw the one
outside me stand for my own, like Dante himself
in Paradise. I felt I was standing inside
the sky, that there were other lights below me
and other worlds and this one could be restored.
And there were other feelings I have forgotten
or can't quite put in words. I saw myself
moving from body to body. I saw my own
existence taken from me. I lost the center.
—It lasted for fifteen minutes, then I slept,
with three or four others, scattered on that roof
as if we each had little rooms, the brilliance
of the night keeping us quiet, all our efforts—
at least my own—going into lying still,
going into some secret humming and adoring,
I was so changed, I was so small and silent.

In Crete the heart gets filled up, there is a joy
there, it is the mountains and sea combined,
it is the knowledge you have that there was a life
there for centuries, half unknown to Europe, half
unknown to Asia, Crete is a kind of moon
to me, a kind of tiny planet,
going through the same revolutions, over and over.
That was the first time I had been in the stars
for maybe twenty years, and it was odd
that I was not in the woods or on the water
in upper Michigan or Maine or Canada,
thousands of miles from civilization, now
it was thousands of years, although it was almost the same.
I dreamed of my bus ride back, some perfect village

in the mountains, and I dreamed of staring through the window
at some small child in blue or smiling at a man
with huge boots on. I wanted to sit in the square,
what little square there was, and talk again
about the ancient cities and the forest
that once filled Crete before I returned again
to my little room on the roof and my crazy pillow
and my sky of bitter lovers and animals,
three hundred miles from Africa, from Egypt.

It wasn't lost on me that it was Dante's
Café that I was sitting in—a coffee house
in Greenwich Village with an overblown photo
of Florence on the wall, squeezed in among
my loved ones, reading books, or talking, or waiting
for someone to come, for someone new to walk in
and catch our interest, the irony—even the comedy—
wasn't lost on me. I think I had been there
over an hour frowning and writing. It was
a disgrace! Thank God for New York! Thank God for tolerance!
Thank God for envy! Except that in New York City
I think there are no heavens, I think you live
without a sky there. I remember one Sunday
a little girl came out to my house in Raubsville,
Pennsylvania. I don't remember her mother.
The girl was black, the mother was white, after
supper we went outside to look at the sky
and smell the river; the girl was terrified
when she saw the stars; we had to take her inside
and hold her, and love her; she had never seen the sky
except in New York, it was half sad, half horrible.
I remember one night on a hill in Pittsburgh
we tried to look at the stars; we had the charts
in front of us—no one would ever laugh
at either my rages or my fantasies
if he had spent *his* twenty years in Pittsburgh
looking for kindness in that rotten sky.
—My left hand is tying my folder, my right hand is helping.
I am getting ready to leave, I look for
a tip, I touch my hat, I am still living
a little in the age of politeness. I walk
through the cement playground at Sixth and Houston and down
to Vandam Street. My poem is over. My life
is on an even keel, though who's to say
when I will waver again. I start to call

my friends up one at a time to talk about the stars,
my friends on the Upper West Side and my friends in the Village,
my friends in New Jersey and Brooklyn. I listen to them rave,
those poor stargazers, everyone with a story,
everyone either a mystic or a poet,
one a musician, one an astrologer,
all of them illuminated, all of them ecstatic,
every one changed, for a minute, by his own memory.

RED BIRD

FOR GREG PAPE AND MARNIE PRANGE

Now I feel safe,
I've gotten my cardinal back again.
I'm standing in Tuscaloosa,
watching her hop through the puddles.
I'm watching her eat and drink, a brown-chested
queen, living outdoors in sweetness and light
with a loose and rotten sparrow as her playmate,
some common thing not fit to touch her hem,
not fit to live with her in the same puddle.

I have to walk over a sick dog to see them,
and through some bicycles and cardboard boxes.
One has a heavy beak and a scarlet headpiece
and one has ruffled feathers and a black throat.
As long as there is a cardinal in my life
I can go anywhere; she was the bird
that, as it turned out, freed me fifteen years
ago in a town in western Pennsylvania
in some unbearable secret rite involving
a withered pear tree and a patented furnace.
There is a pear tree here too, just to add
a little mistiness, and a truck, and a car,
waiting beside the puddle like two kind horses.
But the cardinal now is sweeter and more whimsical
than the last time, maybe a little smaller, and gentler.
I talk and the sparrow flies away, for God knows
what kind of seed or God knows from what kind
            of shadow.
Someone will say, as he always does, this sparrow
is English, you know, you have to make a distinction
between him and our own, he is the sloppiest
sparrow of all, he is aggressive and promiscuous,
just as he lands on the pear tree, just as he lands
on the roof of the truck, and someone will say, it is
a female cardinal, the male is redder, his chest
is bigger and brighter, just as she lands on the car
and just as she disappears, a little speck
somewhere, a kind of messenger, her throat

abounding with information, little farewells
to the English sparrow, little bows to the scholars
with bird-stuff on their brains and beautiful cries—
something between a metallic chirp and a whistle—
to the one from Pennsylvania, the one who loves her.

ADLER

The Jewish King Lear is getting ready
for some kind of horror—he is whispering
in the ears of Regan and Goneril: I know
the past, I know the future, my little hovel

will be in Pennsylvania, I will be
an old man eating from a newspaper,
I will stop to read the news, my fish
will soak the petty world up, it will stretch

from Sears on the left to Gimbels on the right,
my table will be a crate and I will cover
the little spaces with tape, it is enough
for my thin elbows. They will look at him

with hatred reminiscent of the Plains
of Auschwitz—Buchenwald—and drive him mad
an inch at a time. Nothing either in England
or Germany could equal his ferocity,

could equal his rage, even if the Yiddish
could make you laugh. There is a famous picture
of a German soldier plucking a beard; I think
of gentle Gloucester every time I see

that picture. There is a point where even Yiddish
becomes a tragic tongue and even Adler
can make you weep. They sit in their chairs for hours
to hear him curse his God; he looks at the dust

and asks, What have I done, what have I done,
for Him to turn on me; that audience murmurs,
Daughters, daughters, it cries for the sadness that came
to all of them in America. King Lear,

may the Lord keep him, hums in agony,
he is a monster of suffering, so many holes
that he is more like a whistle than like a king,
and yet when sometimes he comes across the stage

crowned with burdocks and nettles and cuckoo flowers
we forget it is Adler, we are so terrified,
we are so touched by pity. It is said
that Isadora Duncan came to worship him,

that John Barrymore came to study his acting,
that when he died they carried his coffin around
from theater to theater, that people mourned in the streets,
that he lay in a Windsor tie and a black silk coat.

One time he carried Cordelia around in his arms
he almost forgot his words, he was so moved
by his own grief, there were tears and groans
for him when they remembered his misfortune.

I thank God they were able to weep
and wring their hands for Lear, and sweet Cordelia,
that it happened almost forty years
before our hell, that there was still time then

to walk out of the theater in the sunlight
and discuss tragedy on the bright sidewalk
and live a while by mercy and innocence
with a king like Adler keeping the tremors alive

in their voices and the tears brimming in their eyes.
Thank God they died so early, that they were buried
one at a time, each with his own service,
that they were not lined up beside the trucks

or the cattle cars. I think when they saw him put
a feather over her lips they were relieved
to see her dead. I think they knew her life
was the last claim against him—the last delusion,

one or two would say. Now he was free,
now he was fully changed, he was *created*,
which is something they could have to talk about
going back to their stairways and their crowded tables

with real streaks of remorse on their faces—
more than forty years, almost fifty,
before the dead were dragged from their places
and dumped on the ground or put in orderly piles—

I think they used a broom on the charred faces
to see if there was breath—and a match or two
was dropped on the naked bodies. For the sake of art
there always was a German or Ukrainian

walking around like a dignified Albany,
or one made sad repentant noises like Kent
and one was philosophical like Edgar,
giving lectures to the burning corpses,

those with gold in their mouths, and those with skin
the color of yellow roses, and those with an arm
or a hand that dropped affectionately on another,
and those whose heads were buried, and those whose black tongues—

as if there were mountains, as if there were cold water
flowing through the ravines, as if there were wine cups
sitting on top of the barrels, as if there were flowers—
still sang in bitterness, still wept and warbled in sorrow.

THE EXPULSION

I'm working like a dog here, testing my memory,
my mouth is slightly open, my eyes are closed,
my hand is lying under the satin pillow.
My subject is loss, the painter is Masaccio,
the church is the Church of the Carmine, the narrow panel
is on the southwest wall, I make a mouth
like Adam, I make a mouth like Eve, I make
a sword like the angel's. Or Schubert; I hear him howling
too, there is a touch of the Orient
throughout the great C Major. I'm thinking again
of poor Jim Wright and the sheet of tissue paper
he sent me. Lament, lament, for the underlayer
of wallpaper, circa 1935.
Lament for the Cretans, how did they disappear?
Lament for Hannibal. I'm standing again
behind some wires, there are some guns, my hand
is drawing in the eyes, I'm making the stripes,
I'm lying alone with water falling down
the left side of my face. That was our painting.
We stood in line to see it, we loved the cry
that came from Eve's black mouth, we loved the grief
of her slanted eyes, we loved poor Adam's face
half buried in his hands, we loved the light
on the shoulder and thighs, we loved the shadows, we loved
the perfect sense of distance. Lament, lament,
for my sister. It took ten years for the flesh to go,
she would be twenty then, she would be sixty
in 1984. Lament for my father,
he died in Florida, he died from fear, apologizing
to everyone around him. I walked through three feet
of snow to buy a suit; it took a day
to get to the airport. Lament, lament. He had
thirty-eight suits, and a bronze coffin; he lay
with his upper body showing, a foot of carpet.
He came to America in 1905, huge wolves
snapped at the horse's legs, the snow was on the ground
until the end of April. The angel is red,
her finger is pointing, she floats above the gate,
her face is cruel, she isn't like the angels
of Blake, or Plato, she is an angry mother,

her wings are firm. Lament, lament, my father
and I are leaving Paradise, an angel
is shouting, my hand is on my mouth, my father
is on the edge of his bed, he uses a knife
for a shoe horn, he is in Pittsburgh, the sky is black,
the air is filthy, he bends half over to squeeze
his foot into his shoe, his eyes are closed,
he's moaning. I miss our paradise, the pool
of water, the flowers. Our lives are merging, our shoes
are not that different. The angel is rushing by,
her lips are curled, there is a coldness, even
a madness to her, Adam and Eve are roaring,
the whole thing takes a minute, a few seconds,
and we are left on somebody's doorstep, one of
my favorites, three or four marble steps and a simple
crumbling brick—it could be Baltimore,
it could be Pittsburgh, the North Side or the Hill.
Inside I know there is a hall to the left
and a living room to the right; no one has modernized
it yet, there are two plum trees in the back
and a narrow garden, cucumbers and tomatoes.
We talk about Russia, we talk about the garden,
we talk about Truman, and Reagan. Our hands are rubbing
the dusty marble, we sit for an hour. "It is
a crazy life," I say, "after all the model
homes we looked at, I come back to the old
row house, I do it over and over." "My house"—
he means his father's—"had a giant garden
and we had peppers and radishes; my sister
Jenny made the pickles." We start to drift
at 5 o'clock in the evening, the cars from downtown
are starting to poison us. It is a paradise
of two, maybe, two at the most, the name
on the mailbox I can't remember, the garden
is full of glass, there is a jazzy door
on the next house over, and louvered windows. It is
a paradise, I'm sure of it. I kiss
him goodbye, I hold him, almost like the kiss
in 1969, in Philadelphia,
the last time I saw him, in the Russian manner,
his mouth against my mouth, his arms around me—
we could do that once before he died—
the huge planes barely lifting off the ground,
the families weeping beside us, the way they do,
the children waving goodbye, the lovers smiling,

the way they do, all our loss, everything
we know of loneliness there, their minds already
fixed on the pain, their hands already hanging,
under the shining windows, near the yellow tiles,
the secret rooms, the long and brutal corridor
down which we sometimes shuffle, and sometimes run.

JULY 2, 1983

This is what it's come to on my primrose path,
a delphinium growing out of a cabbage,
a hosta
or August lily.

This is what a July day looks like
in the 1980s,
a white butterfly,
a shimmer of heat, a shadow.

O ugliest of flowers,
be with me forever,
now that I've lifted my left hand against the tubers,
now that I've lifted my right hand against the motor boats.

O mugho pine,
bless my swallows,
flying madly in and out of their woven duplex,
living for two great weeks with heartbreak and wrangling and terror
and a minute and a half of sleep, and a minute and a half of silence.

LOVESICK

THE DOG

What I was doing with my white teeth exposed
like that on the side of the road I don't know,
and I don't know why I lay beside the sewer
so that lover of dead things could come back
with his pencil sharpened and his piece of white paper.
I was there for a good two hours whistling
dirges, shrieking a little, terrifying
hearts with my whimpering cries before I died
by pulling the one leg up and stiffening.
There is a look we have with the hair of the chin
curled in mid-air, there is a look with the belly
stopped in the midst of its greed. The lover of dead things
stoops to feel me, his hand is shaking. I know
his mouth is open and his glasses are slipping.
I think his pencil must be jerking and the terror
of smell—and sight—is overtaking him;
I know he has that terrified faraway look
that death brings—he is contemplating. I want him
to touch my forehead once and rub my muzzle
before he lifts me up and throws me into
that little valley. I hope he doesn't use
his shoe for fear of touching me; I know,
or used to know, the grasses down there; I think
I knew a hundred smells. I hope the dog's way
doesn't overtake him, one quick push,
barely that, and the mind freed, something else,
some other thing, to take its place. Great heart,
great human heart, keep loving me as you lift me,

give me your tears, great loving stranger, remember
the death of dogs, forgive the yapping, forgive
the shitting, let there be pity, give me your pity.
How could there be enough? I have given
my life for this, emotion has ruined me, oh lover,
I have exchanged my wildness—little tricks
with the mouth and feet, with the tail, my tongue is a parrot's,
I am a rampant horse, I am a lion,
I wait for the cookie, I snap my teeth—
as you have taught me, oh distant and brilliant and lonely.

LOVESICK

The dead straw in those trees, the
dead leaves in those trees
have turned to birds, they have turned
to crows, they are watching a deer
or a piece of tire, my foot
is on the deer's black head,
my face is in the clouds,
I kick the tire over
to see the guts. I want
the whole thing for myself.
They want the eyes, they want
the stinking shoulder, they wait
for me to leave, I kick
the legs, I drag them across
the highway, all those beaks
are snapping, all those tails
are waving in the wind,
their bellies are moaning and howling,
their souls are cooing and cawing.

ALL I HAVE ARE THE TRACKS

All I have are the tracks. There were a dog's
going down the powdered steps, there was a woman
going one way, a man going the other, a squirrel
on top of the man; sometimes his paws were firm,
the claws were showing—in fear, in caution—sometimes
they sort of scurried, then sort of leaped. The prints
go east and west; there is a boot; there is
a checkerboard style, a hexagram style; my own
I study now, my Georgia Loggers, the heel
a kind of target, the sole a kind of sponge;
the tiny feet are hopping, four little paws,
the distance between them is fifteen inches, they end
in the grass, in the leaves, there are four toes and a palm,
the nose isn't there, the tail isn't there, the teeth
that held the acorn, the eyes that thought; and the hands
that held the books, and the face that froze, and the shoulders
that fought the wind, and the mouth that struggled for air,
and love and hate, and all their shameless rages.

I DO A PIECE FROM GREECE

I do a piece from Greece. I haven't done that
for three or four years. I turn the radio up.
I stare at my ties. I pick a California
and wrap it around my robe. There is a shark
on the ceiling above my shoes. Her nose is pointed
toward the door. She is the streamlined body
we dreamed about in the thirties. Her tail is monstrous,
her brain is a pea. I pluck the strings
in a kind of serenade. I raise the bow
above my head and bend a little, my hair
is hanging down. I am at last the musician
my mother wanted. My aunts and uncles are sitting
on wooden boxes, they are sobbing and sighing,
I take my time, I have a Schubert to go.
I have a light beside me. I am lying
under the Sea of Azov, it is a joy
to be here, they are howling. I raise my elbow
to make a sound. I wait for the moon to shine
on the Allegheny. I look at their faces, they turn
the pages, eleven uncles and aunts, a leather
coffin. I start to play, it is the only
way I have of weeping, it is my way
of joining them, my tears were taken away
when I was eight, this way we end up singing
together. I am a note above them, it is
the thirteenth century, singing in fifths, in parts
of the south they sing like that; the violin rises
above the alto, a shrieking sound, we humans
shriek at the end, we want so much to be heard.
My way was with the soaring and the singing.
Once I heard it I could never stop.

THIS WAS A WONDERFUL NIGHT

This was a wonderful night. I heard the Brahms
piano quintet, I read a poem by Schiller,
I read a story, I listened to *Gloomy Sunday*.
No one called me, I studied the birthday poem
of Alvaro de Campos. I thought, if there was time,
I'd think of my garden—all that lettuce, wasted,
all those huge tomatoes lying on the ground
rotting, and I'd think of the sticks I put there,
waving goodbye, those bearded sticks. De Campos,
he was the one who suffered most, his birthday
was like a knife to him; he sat in a chair
remembering his aunts; he thought of the flowers
and cakes, he thought of the sideboard crowded with gifts.
I look at the photo of Billie Holiday;
I turn the light bulb on and off. I envy
those poets who loved their childhood, those who remember
the extra places laid out, the china and glasses.
They want to devour the past, they revel in pity,
they live like burnt-out matches, memory ruins them;
again and again they go back to the first place.

De Campos and I are sitting on a bench
in some American city. He hardly knows
how much I love his country. I have two things
to tell him about my childhood, one is the ice
on top of the milk, one is the sign in the window—
three things—the smell of coal. There is some snow
left on the street, the wind is blowing. He trembles
and touches the buttons on his vest. His house
is gone, his aunts are dead, the tears run down
our cheeks and chins, we are like babies, crying.
"Leave thinking to the head," he says. I sob,
"I don't have birthdays any more," I say,
"I just go on," although I hardly feel
the sadness, there is such joy in being there
on that small bench, watching the sycamores,
looking for birds in the snow, listening for boots,
staring at the begonias, getting up
and down to rub the leaves and touch the buds—
endless pleasure, talking about New York,

comparing pain, writing the names down
of all the cities south of Lisbon, singing
one or two songs—a hundred years for him,
a little less for me, going east and west
in the new country, my heart forever pounding.

I SOMETIMES THINK OF THE LAMB

I sometimes think of the lamb when I crawl down
my flight of stairs, my back is twisted sideways
in a great arc of pain from the shoulder down
and the buttocks up. I think of the lamb through my tears
as I go down a step at a time, my left hand
squeezing the rail, my right hand holding my thigh
and lifting it up. As long as there is a lamb
I can get on my hands and knees if I have to
and walk across the floor like a limp wolf,
and I can get my body to the sink
and lift myself up to the white porcelain.
As long as there is a lamb, as long as he lives
in his brown pen or his green meadow,
as long as he kneels on the platform staring at the light,
surrounded by men and women with raised fingers,
as long as he has that little hump on his rear
and that little curve to his tail, as long as his foot
steps over the edge in terror and ignorance,
as long as he holds a cup to his own side,
as long as he is stabbed and venerated,
as long as there are hooves—and clattering—
as long as there is screaming and butchering.

STOPPING SCHUBERT

Stopping Schubert, ejecting him, changing the power,
I make it from Newark to the shores of Oberlin
in less than nine hours, Schubert roaring and groaning
halfway there, the violins in the mountains,
the cellos in the old state forests.
When I reach Clarion I know I am near Pittsburgh.
I turn the tape down; I can live off the music
of childhood for a while—I still know the words
in both languages—I am not that different
even today. My mouth makes a humming sound
just as it did back then. I take my comb out
and my piece of paper. I bang the swollen dashboard
thinking of my golden trombone; I ruined
the lives of twenty-four families in those days
sliding from note to note, it was my fate
not to make a sound on the French horn,
to rage on my trombone. I still love Schubert
most of all, *Death and the Maiden, Frozen Tears,*
Der Lindenbaum.
I have kept it a secret for forty years,
the tortured composer from central Pennsylvania,
Franz Schubert.

I AM IN A WINDOW

I move from chair to chair. Thinking of Liszt.
I am in a certain century again
going from city to city. I am in a window
with Berlioz on my left and Czerny on my right;
Liszt is looking into the clouds, his wrists
seem to be waiting. I am in an oil painting.
Victor Hugo is there, and Paganini,
and Sand and Dumas side by side. A bust
of Beethoven is half sitting on the piano,
half sitting in the sky. We live by the light
of Saint-Simon—it is our socialism,
freedom from rage, freedom from marriage,
freedom from money; or it is Weimar
forty years later, Liszt is at the window,
Wagner has come and gone, the world is whistling
Brahms and Debussy; in a few years
Gandhi will be born, then Frank Lloyd Wright.
The continent has shifted half an inch,
a little joy has come to Zuyder Zee,
a little horror has come to the Crimea.
I move from table to table, from room to room,
I try to think of Gurdjieff, what was the work
he had in store for me? Where were the shovels?
I think of Rudolf Steiner, all the reading
he did on Hegel and Goethe; I think of the gatherings
in Switzerland, and France, I see his hand
in a book, his eyes are radiant. I pack
my bag, a leather strap, a leather pocket—
how well the goods were made in 1910,
fifteen years before my birth—my soul
was probably born too late, it had a certain
zest, I think, for the wrong century
and fluttered along for decade after decade
with the wrong digits—that is the way it is
with souls—I have a rug upstairs to roll in,
something to keep me warm, it came from Crete
and has three green and yellow flowers on it,
on a field of crimson; I bought it in Chania.
I'll lie there for hours thinking of my mountains,
reading Keats.

BÉLA

This version of the starving artist
has him composing his last concerto
while dying of leukemia. Serge Koussevitsky
visits him in his hospital room
with flowers in his hand, the two of them
talk in tones of reverence, the last
long piece could be the best, the rain somewhere
makes daring noises, somewhere clouds are bursting.
I have the record in front of me. I drop
the needle again on the famous ending, five
long notes, then all is still, I have to imagine
two great seconds of silence and then applause
and shouting, he is in tears, Koussevitsky
leads him onto the stage. Or he is distant,
remembering the mountains, there in Boston
facing the wild Americans, he closes
his eyes so he can hear another note,
something from Turkey, or Romania, his mother
holding his left hand, straightening out the fingers,
he bows from the waist, he holds his right hand up.
I love the picture with Benny Goodman, Szigetti
is on the left, Goodman's cheeks are puffed
and his legs are crossed. Bartók is at the piano.
They are rehearsing Bartók's *Contrasts*. I lift
my own right hand, naturally I do that;
I listen to my blood, I touch my wrist.
If he could have only lived for three more years
he could have heard about our Mussolini
and seen the violent turn to the right and the end
of one America and the beginning of another.
That would have given him time enough to brood
on Hungary; that would have given him time
also to go among the Indians
and learn their music, and listen to their chants,
those tribes from Michigan and Minnesota,
just like the tribes of the Finns and the Urgo-Slavics,
moaning and shuffling in front of their wooden tents.

There is a note at the end of the second movement
I love to think about; it parodies

Shostakovitch; it is a kind of flutter
of the lips. And there is a note—I hear it—
of odd regret for a life not lived enough,
everyone knows that sound, for me it's remorse,
and there is a note of crazy satisfaction,
this I love, of the life he would not change
no matter what—no other animal
could have such pleasure. I think of this as I turn
the music off, and I think of his poor eyes
as they turned to ice—his son was in the room
and saw the change—I call it a change. Bartók
himself lectured his friends on death, it was
his woods and mountain lecture, fresh green shoots
pushing up through the old, the common home
that waits us all, the cycles, the laws of nature,
wonderfully European, all life and death
at war—peacefully—one thing replacing another,
although he grieved over cows and pitied dogs
and listened to pine cones as if they came from the sea
and fretted over the smallest of life.

He died

September 28, 1945,
just a month after the war was over.
It took him sixty days to finish the piece
from the time he lay there talking to Koussevitsky
to the time he put a final dot on the paper,
a little pool of ink to mark the ending.
There are the five loud notes, I walk upstairs
to hear them, I put a silk shawl over my head
and rock on the wooden floor, the shawl is from France
and you can see between the threads; I feel
the darkness, I was born with a veil over
my eyes, it took me forty years to rub
the gum away, it was a blessing, I sit
for twenty minutes in silence, daylight is coming,
the moon is probably near, probably lifting
its satin nightgown, one hand over the knee
to hold the cloth up so the feet can walk
through the wet clouds; I love that bent-over motion,
that grace at the end of a long and furious night.
I go to sleep on the floor, there is a pillow
somewhere for my heavy head, my hand
is resting on the jacket, Maazel is leading
the Munich orchestra, a nurse is pulling
the sheet up, Bartók is dead, his wife is walking

past the sun room, her face is white, her mind
is on the apartment they lost, where she would put
the rugs, how she would carry in his breakfast,
where they would read, her mind is on Budapest,
she plays the piano for him, she is eighteen
and he is thirty-seven, he is gone
to break the news, she waits in agony,
she goes to the telephone; I turn to the window,
I stare at my palm, I draw a heart in the dust,
I put the arrow through it, I place the letters
one inside the other. I sleep, I sleep.

A SONG FOR THE ROMEOS*

FOR MY BROTHERS
JIM WRIGHT AND DICK HUGO

I'm singing a song for the romeos
I wore for ten years on my front stoop in the North Side,
and for the fat belly I carried
and the magic ticket sticking out of my greasy hatband
or my vest pocket,
the green velvet one with the checkered borders
and the great stretched back with the tan ribs
going west and east like fishes of the deep looking for their covers.

I'm wearing my romeos
with the papery thin leather
and the elastic side bands.
They are made for sitting,
or a little walking into the kitchen and out,
a little tea in the hands,
a little Old Forester or a little Schenley in the tea.

I'm singing a song for the corner store
and the empty shelves;
for the two blocks of flattened buildings
and broken glass;
for the streetcar that still rounds the bend
with sparks flying through the air.

And the woman with a shopping bag,
and the girl with a book
walking home one behind the other,
their steps half dragging, half ringing,
the romeos keeping time,
tapping and knocking and clapping on the wooden steps
and the cement sidewalk.

*Romeos were a kind of indoor/outdoor slipper or sandal.

A SLOW AND PAINFUL
RECOVERY

Richard Strauss, my hero, here you are
finally letting go of both sword and breast,
and there you are escaping from our bleeding world
onto a mountain or into a cloud. I stare
at the pink fixture, it is a flattened breast
with a longish nipple, breasts half over the world
are covering light bulbs, there is a light bulb out
and a darkened breast in the other room; I stay here
with my lilacs and daisies, I am in my bed
of needles. Now it's Schumann again, the second,
his deep depression gone by the final movement,
and soon it will be Mozart, Europe again,
the true Europe, lilacs everywhere,
the cellos of the plant world. This is the last
good day for the first bouquet. I know there are some
daisies left among the lilies. The second
bouquet is better, it refuses to bow,
it brings the outside in, I think it's the bluebell,
I think it's the red bud crawling and twisting, a kind of
Japanese dancing, maybe more formal than twisting.

I'm writing the fourteenth now. I'm doing it
in a room with all my boxes and boots and paintings.
I'm getting ready to move. My bed of needles—
crooked, antique—is in the midst of it all.
Each day I walk a mile, I crawl and twist
like a broken branch, I pass the scented tree,
I pass the poppies, I pass the lilacs, I climb
two giant hills, my face is twisted, I hold
the rusted rail—this house is historical—
and pull myself up the steps. My crisis was the spine,
one or two flattened discs, I had the pain,
I had the depression, I had the boredom. There are
paths I know that no one knows. I know
the color of tulips in every yard. I know
the sheets of green with yellow discs. I watch them
turn white. I know a house so small the owners
are either midgets with squeaky voices or giants

with little chairs and tables, little beds
they and their children play in. There is a mailbox
nailed onto the shingles. There is a railing
falling over—the giants' heavy touch,
the midgets' swinging. There is a small backyard
with white and purple lilacs. I am listening
to Haydn's sixty-sixth, the ever loyal
Haydn, Haydn the good, Ben Franklin Haydn.
I take my pills—daily at bedtime—I look at
my Cretan rug. I fought for days to save
five or ten dollars, every day the dealer
sent out for coffee, every day he told me
about his life in Chicago and every day
we struggled in silence. I turn the lights out, my mind
is all alone, it begs for Valium, it cries
for milk and scotch. At four in the morning the birds
and I are screaming. I start my long walk at five;
the shadows let me alone, the perfume tree
is silent, my hands are shaking—a little residual
weakness—my leg is dragging, I turn the corner
to a kind of dawn, there is a weak light over
the sycamores—the perfume tree is apple—
the red bud is split in two, the poppies are opening.
It was a slow and painful recovery.

MY FIRST KINGLET

I saw my first kinglet in Iowa City
on Sunday, April twenty-second, 1984,
flying from tree to tree, and bush to bush.
She had a small yellow patch on her stomach,
a little white around her eyes. I reached
for a kiss, still dumb and silent as always. I put
a finger out for a branch and opened my hand
for a kind of clearing in the woods, a wrinkled
nest you'd call it, half inviting, half
disgusting maybe, or terrifying, a pink
and living nest. The kinglet stood there singing
"A Mighty Fortress Is Our God." She was
a pure Protestant, warbling in the woods,
confessing everything. I said goodbye,
a friend of all the Anabaptists, a friend
of all the Lutherans. I cleared my throat
and off she went for some other pink finger
and some other wrinkled palm. I started to whistle,
but only to the trees; my kinglet was gone
and her pipe was gone and her yellow crown was gone,
and I was left with only a spiral notebook
and the end of a pencil. I was good and careful,
for all I had left of the soul was in that stub,
a wobbling hunk of lead embedded in wood,
pine probably—pencils are strange—I sang
another Protestant hymn; the lead was loose
and after a minute I knew I'd just be holding
the blunt and slippery end. That was enough
for one Sunday. I thanked the trees, I thanked
the tulips with their six red tongues. I lay
another hour, another hour; I either
slept a little or thought a little. Life—
it could have been a horror, it could have been
gory and full of pain. I ate my sandwich
and waited for a signal, then I began
my own confession; I walked on the stones, I sighed
under a hemlock, I whistled under a pine,
and reached my own house almost out of breath
from walking too fast—from talking too loud—
from waving my arms and beating my palms; I was,

for five or ten minutes, one of those madmen you see
forcing their way down Broadway, reasoning with themselves
the way a squirrel does, the way a woodpecker does,
half dressed in leaf, half dressed in light, my dear face
appearing and disappearing, my heavy legs
with their shortened hamstrings tripping a little, a yard
away from my wooden steps and my rusty rail,
the thicket I lived in for two years, more or less,
Dutch on one side, American Sioux on the other,
Puerto Rican and Bronx Hasidic inside,
a thicket fit for a king or a wandering kinglet.

LILLIAN HARVEY

This is lovesick for you—Charles Koechlin
covering his paper with tears, he shushes his wife
and his children, he is crying for Lillian Harvey—
or this is lovesick—sending his wife to meet her,
he is too shy to go, and he is married;
when she comes back he asks a thousand questions:
What was she wearing? Does she like his music?
How old did she look? Was she like her photograph?
But he never met her, she whose face haunted him,
although he wrote a hundred and thirteen compositions
for her, including two *Albums for Lillian*,
and he wrote a film scenario and score,
which he imagined, fantastically,
would star the two of them. He was himself
twice in America, both times in California,
but they couldn't meet—it would be a violation.
I know that agony myself, I stood
on one foot or another four or five times
and burned with shame and shook with terror. You never
go yourself. I know he must have waited
outside her house, a crazy man, he must have
dialed her number a hundred times, even risked
his life for her. But you never go, you never
stand there smiling—he never stood there smiling,
he never reached his hand inside her dress,
he never touched her nipple, he never pressed
his mouth against her knee or lifted her thighs.
For she was the muse. You never fuck the muse.

THERE I WAS ONE DAY

There I was one day
in the parking lot of the First Brothers' Church
on one foot, a giant whooping crane
with my left ibex finger against my temple
trying to remember what my theory of corruption was
and why I got so angry years ago
at my poor mother and father, immigrant cranes
from Polish Russia and German and Jewish Ukraine—
the good days then, hopping both ways like a frog,
and croaking, and trying to remember why it was
I soothed myself with words
at that flimsy secretary, not meant for knees,
not meant for a soul, not least a human one,
and trying to remember how I pieced together
the great puzzle, and how delighted I was
I would never again be bitten twice,
on either hand, the left one or the other.
I stopped between the telephone pole and the ivy
and sang to myself. I do it now for pleasure.
I thought I'd trace the line of pure decadence
to either Frank Sinatra or Jackie Gleason,
and thence to either the desert or the swamp,
Greater Nevada or Miami Beach;
or I would smile with Stalin or frown with Frick,
Stalin and Frick, both from Pittsburgh; Mellon,
Ehrlichman, Paul the Fortieth, Paul the Fiftieth.
I learned my bitterness at the dining room table
and used it everywhere. One time I yanked
the tablecloth off with everything on top of it.
It was the kind of strength that lets you lift
the back end of a car, it was the rush
of anger and righteousness you shake from later.
My Polish mother and my Ukrainian father
sat there white-faced. They had to be under fifty,
maybe closer to forty. I had hit them
between the eyes, I had screamed in their ears
and spit in their faces. Forty years later I stutter
when I think about it; it is the stuttering
of violent justice. I turned left on Third—
it was called Pomfret in 1776—

and made my way to the square—I think I did that—
past the Plaza II and the old Huntington,
and did an Egyptian turn. There were some other birds
sitting there on the benches, eating egg salad
and smoking autumn leaves. They didn't seem to care
or even notice. We sat there for the humming
and later we left, one at a time, and limped
away at different speeds, in different directions.
I ended up doing a circle, east on one street,
north on another, past the round oak table
in the glass window, past the swimming pool
at the YW. Just a walk for me
is full of exhaustion; nobody does it my way,
shaking the left foot, holding the right foot up,
a stork from Broadway, a heron from Mexico,
a pink flamingo from Greece.

ONE ANIMAL'S LIFE

FOR ROSALIND PACE

This is how I saved one animal's life,
I raised the lid of the stove and lifted the hook
that delicately held the cheese—I think it was bacon—
so there could be goodness and justice under there.
It was a thirty-inch range with the pilot lit
in the center of two small crosses. It was a Wincroft
with a huge oven and two flat splash pans above it.
The four burners were close together, it was
a piece of white joy, from 1940 I'd judge
from the two curved handles, yet not as simple as
my old Slattery, not as sleek. I owe
a lot to the woman who gave me this house, she is
a lover of everything big and small, she moans
for certain flowers and insects, I hear her snuffle
all night sometimes, I hear her groan. She gave me
a bed and a kitchen, she gave me music, I couldn't be
disloyal to her, yet I had to lift
the murderous hook. I'll hear her lectures later
on *my* inconsistencies and hypocrisies;
I'll struggle in the meantime, like everyone else, to make
my way between the stove and refrigerator
without sighing or weeping too much. Mice
are small and ferocious. If I killed one it wouldn't be
with poison or traps. I couldn't just use our weapons
without some compensation. I'd have to be present—
if it was a trap—and hear it crash and lift
the steel myself and look at the small flat nose
or the small crushed head, I'd have to hold the pallet
and drop the body into a bag. I ask
forgiveness of butchers and hunters; I'm starting to talk
to vegetarians now, I'm reading books,
I'm washing my icebox down with soda and lye,
I'm buying chicory, I'm storing beans.
I should have started this thirty years ago,
holding my breath, eating ozone, starving,
sitting there humming, feeling pure and indignant
beside the chewed-up bags and the black droppings.

SILVER HAND

There is that little silver hand. I wrap
my fingers around the wrist. I press my thumb
on the shiny knuckles. There is a little slot
in the empty palm—the lines are crude and lifeless,
more like an ape's hand, more like a child's, no hope
for the future of any kind, a life line dragging
its way through civilization, the line of destiny
faint and broken, a small abandoned road,
the heart line short, no sweetness, no ecstasy,
and no dear journeys, and no great windfalls. I shake
the wrist, there are some dimes and nickels inside,
but it is mostly empty, an empty hand
reaching out. It is the hand that acts
for the spirit, there is a connection, the hand has mercy,
the hand is supple and begs, the hand is delicate,
even if it is brutal sometimes, even if it is evil—
and it is penniless and lost, a true
spirit, that sings a little and dances a little,
green or shiny on the outside, black on the inside.
Give to the hand!

WASHINGTON SQUARE

Now after all these years I am just that one pigeon
limping over towards that one sycamore tree
with my left leg swollen and my left claw bent and my neck
just pulling me along. It is the annual
day of autumn glory, but I am limping
into the shade of that one sycamore tree.
Forget about Holley crumbling out there in the square,
forget about Garibaldi in his little hollow;
remember one pigeon, white and grey, with a touch
of the old blue, his red leg swollen, his claw
dragging him on and on, the sickness racking
his skinny neck; remember the one pigeon
fighting his way through the filthy marijuana,
sighing.

ARRANGING A THORN

I am wandering through Newark, New Jersey,
among the gymnasts, the accountants and the kings
and my arms are breaking from all the weight I carry.
I am wearing the same blue pants and jacket
I have worn for the last twenty years
and mumbling to myself as always
as I go out of one long corridor and into another
or up an escalator
and into a jazzy bar
or through the beeper, over and over again,
discarding my metal, dropping my keys and watches.
I am ranked below the businessmen
with their two-suiters and their glasses of ice
and I get a slightly bored or slightly disdainful look
from the flight attendants and the drunken crew
and the food gatherers.
This is the trip I'm going to think about Rexroth
and what it was like in 1959
reading his poem on murdered poets,
and Shelley's *Adonais*
and Dunbar's *Lament*,
half a dirge for Dunbar,
half a dirge for the reader, sick and dying.
—Ah brother Levine and brother Stanley Plumly,
what hell we live in; we travel from Tuscaloosa
to Houston; we go to Chicago; we meet the monster
and spend our night at the Richmont or the Hyatt,
there is a table by the bed, the rug
on the wall is there to ruin us, coffee and toast
is seven dollars. Murphy meets us in leather
at the South Street station and drives us over a curb;
I pay for my own meal; twenty people show up
for the reading; it is the night that Carter loses;
my back is out of place. It was in the *Ion*
that Plato doomed the poets. There is no peace
in any land, we stand in the dust and kick
our shoes, some with holes in the toes and some
with holes in the soles. That's all there is. The prizes
are there for delusion. Oh brother Ignatow, oh br'er
Bly, there is such joy in sitting here knowing

one thing from another; I feel like singing;
that darkness is gone, that angry blackness. I sort
the leaves, my life is full of leaves again,
I make a garland for my head, it is
a garland of pity—I won't say glory—poets
are full of pity, I talk to them, they hate to
think about glory, it is the terror, everything
lost, their poems shredded and burned, their music
boring, or insignificant, or derivative,
a critic somewhere keeping time, but *pity*,
pity is for this life, pity is the worm
inside the meat, pity is the meat, pity
is the shaking pencil, pity is the shaking voice—
not enough money, not enough love—pity
for all of us—it is our grace, walking
down the ramp or on the moving sidewalk,
sitting in a chair, reading the paper, pity,
turning a leaf to the light, arranging a thorn.

A PAIR OF HANDS

That is a pair of white hands I see
floating in the mirror, the fingers on the left
are blunt and rounded, the ones on the right are raised
as if in thought. They are almost like gloves,
the lines are gone, they are abstracted, the suffering
is in the creases, somewhere in the folds
underneath the knuckles, or somewhere in the spaces
over the fingertips. I choose them this time
over the mouth, the mouth with two great trenches
and two great cheeks beyond the trenches, the mouth
with a curled smile, and I choose them over the eyes,
surrounded by wrinkles, wounded and bloodshot. The hands
are permanent and heavy, they are the means
both to pain and pleasure, thus the ancient
Peruvians buried them inside their clothes,
thus the Arabs cut them off and fed
them to their dogs. Our age is weak—and vague—
in what it does with hands, there is a history
both of terror and loathing. My first forty years
were an agony. I lived by touching and holding.
It was my ruin.

BOB SUMMERS' BODY

I never told this—I saw Bob Summers' body
one last time when they dropped him down the chute
at the crematorium. He turned over twice
and seemed to hang with one hand to the railing
as if he had to sit up once and scream
before he reached the flames. I was half terrified
and half ashamed to see him collapse like that
just two minutes after we had sung for him
and said our pieces. It was impossible
for me to see him starting another destiny
piled up like that, or see him in that furnace
as one who was being consoled or purified.
If only we had wrapped him in his sheet
so he could be prepared; there is such horror
standing before Persephone with a suit on,
the name of the manufacturer in the lining,
the pants too short, or too long. How hard it was
for poor Bob Summers in this life, how he struggled
to be another person. I hope his voice,
which he lost through a stroke in 1971,
was given back to him, wherever he strayed,
the smell of smoke still on him, the fire lighting up
his wonderful eyes again, his hands explaining,
anyone, god or man, moved by his logic,
spirits in particular, saved by the fire and clasping
their hands around their knees, some still worm-bound,
their noses eaten away, their mouths only dust,
nodding and smiling in the plush darkness.

IT WAS IN HOUSTON

It was in Houston I saw this disgusting sideboard
with dogs and foxes and lobsters carved into
the wood, a giant stag was hanging down
from a polished rope, there was an eagle on top
and bowls of fruit and plates of fish—all carved.
I opened the drawer and put my message inside.
The drawer was smooth and faultless, one of the hidden
ones without knobs, curved and rounded, with nice
round insides that soothe the soul. It might
take a year for someone to open the drawer.
It would be either a mother or her son;
the mother would be mad with cleaning, her fingers
would itch to get at the inside of that furniture
and rub some oil into the corners, the son
would long to take the piece apart, to loosen
the stag, to free the eagle, to find a dime
inside the hidden drawer. This would be before
she turned to books and he turned to motorcycles;
or it would be a musician, someone who loves
to touch old wood. It never would be a poet—
they are all blind—who pulls the drawer and finds
my secret words. For any of these three,
here is the white pen I am writing with,
here is my yellow tablet, there are no
magic thumb prints, nothing that is not there,
only the hum, and I have buried that
on the piece of paper. It is a small envelope;
I always have one in my jacket; the words
are simple, half music, half thought, half tongue, half tear,
and made for the pocket book or the hip pocket,
or the inside of a wallet—I like that best—
folded up, and there are broken words,
or torn, hanging onto the threads, the deep ones
underneath the flap, the dark ones forever creased,
the song half hovering in that cloth lining
as if a moth were struggling out of the leather,
half caught between the money and the poetry,
little white one in the ravaged world.

NEITHER ENGLISH NOR SPANISH

FOR HEIDI KALAFSKI

It was when I went out to get an angry soul
a little cool and a little windy. Some bird
was clacking his beak or maybe rubbing his gums
together either for singing or for crushing
a watery insect. I was driving with one sister
to find another and the car we drove in
was huge and fast and dangerous. I thought
the darkness we drove in was something like daylight although
the lights on the body seemed more like lamps, just lighting
the ten or twelve feet in front of us. It is
the madness of northern New Jersey I'm describing,
a sulphur day and night, a cloud of gas
always hanging above us. We drifted down
to Newark, there were clusters of people in front of
every bar and drug store, they were mostly
very young, as if the population over twenty
had disappeared and the care of life and the care of
the culture were in the hands of babies, all our
wisdom, our history, were in their hands. I stopped
over and over to ask directions, the language
they spoke was neither English nor Spanish, they either
pointed in some odd direction or stood there staring.
I bounced up over the curb into a radiant
gasoline island; there was a psycho-pomp
in a clean white suit who calmed me down and told me
where the phone booth and the park was I wanted.
His English was perfect. I was shocked to see him
in a job like that, reaching over and wiping
the mist away, holding his hand on the pump,
staring at nothing. He should have been a lawyer
or engineer, but he was black, although
he could have been a student. I gave him a tip
and turned around. This time I found the park
in half a minute but there was nothing in sight,
not even a police car with its fat dog yowling
or some stray bleak berserker on the burnt grass.
I locked the car, the other sister sat there
trembling. I tried to smile. I found a dime,
and then a quarter, for my phone call. I stood there
on the sidewalk holding the black receiver

and listening to noisy insects. The sweet life
outside is different from the life of the car.
I suddenly wanted to walk. I wanted to touch
the trees, or sit on the ground. There was a ringing
but no one answered, as I recall. I shouldn't
have made a mystique of that but I was shouting
"bad connection" to myself and "vile connection"
and "fake connection," all that we hold dear
in twentieth-century evil communication.
That was where I could have lifted my fist
and played for the dirty trees, but I was tired
and struggling with the stupid lock, a Ford
Galaxy Superba. Anyhow, I got bored
with the park and its shadows, I did a fainthearted dance,
a mild frenzy on the sidewalk, and sang me
a primitive note, a long moaning note,
as I put my car into "drive," the lever hanging
somewhere in oblivion, the meshes
ruined, no right connection between the orange
letters and the mushy gears.
                                    This was
my futile descent into Newark. We returned
empty-handed, empty-hearted. I smoked
a single cigarette in the blackness and ranted
against New Jersey, as if there was a difference
between one land and another. That dear girl
we looked for would be sitting in the kitchen,
surrounded by her family, thin and exhausted,
full of terror, her mind erasing one horror
after another; and I would hold her and kiss her
along with the others. We would be some tragic
group somewhere, someone would boil water,
and we would talk all night, even end up laughing
a little before the streaks of light and the morning
noises brought us to our senses. I turned
right where I had to turn right and found the buried
driveway as always. I was right, the kitchen
lights were burning and there were cars and trucks
parked wildly in the yard. I looked at the dawn
behind the A&P and the pizzeria—
that takes two seconds in New Jersey—and climbed
over a sled, a tire and an ironing board—
I who saw the dead and knew the music—
and opened the door to that embattled kitchen
and shook hands all around, I and the sister.

I AM IN LOVE

Everyone who dances understands what I am doing,
standing for hours in front of the card catalogue
and walking up and down the black riverbank.
He understands it how I stop and gesture,
that talking to the dead, and how I make
a face for every age, a vile one for ours,
a sweet one for one I half forgot, a wrinkled one
for the one that is Peruvian and a smooth one
for the one that is Egyptian. I have been working
among the O's; I started with Orpheus
and have been there for months; there are some libraries
where you can live in the stacks, you bring your lunch
and sleep on the heated floor. My scholarship
is hectic, I can start with an O and stray
to everything in sight, Pound and paideuma,
Palladio—I steal that from my son—
his trips through Italy, his view of the sky.
There is a dance in which I sit for one hour
with warm milk in my hands, the furnace is roaring
and just outside the window one or two cars
are driving by in the darkness. In it I either
find a book, or I find a piece of paper
and a yellow pencil. I sway a little and moan
all to myself. When I am done, when the milk
is done, I stand and bow to the shopping bag,
to the Sears rug—I have an audience—
and climb the fifteen steps with my head down
and my legs dragging—another dance. I have
a helpless fascination with myself,
I love to watch myself when I climb stairs,
or when I drink that milk. I stay alive
that way, I am amazed at myself. I have
no power over it, whether I'm lying and sleeping
or lying awake and staring. Sometimes I sit
like a stone, I do the lines of wind and rain,
sometimes I do the birch tree searching for the sun,
sometimes I do Route 30. I am in love.

ANOTHER INSANE DEVOTION

This was gruesome—fighting over a ham sandwich
with one of the tiny cats of Rome, he leaped
on my arm and half hung on to the food and half
hung on to my shirt and coat. I tore it apart
and let him have his portion, I think I lifted him
down, sandwich and all, on the sidewalk and sat
with my own sandwich beside him, maybe I petted
his bony head and felt him shiver. I have
told this story over and over; some things
root in the mind; his boldness, of course, was frightening
and unexpected—his stubbornness—though hunger
drove him mad. It was the breaking of boundaries,
the sudden invasion, but not only that, it was
the sharing of food and the sharing of space; he didn't
run into an alley or into a cellar,
he sat beside me, eating, and I didn't run
into a trattoria, say, shaking,
with food on my lips and blood on my cheek, sobbing;
but not only that, I had gone there to eat
and wait for someone. I had maybe an hour
before she would come and I was full of hope
and excitement. I have resisted for years
interpreting this, but now I think I was given
a clue, or I was giving myself a clue,
across the street from the glass sandwich shop.
That was my last night with her, the next day
I would leave on the train for Paris and she would
meet her husband. Thirty-five years ago
I ate my sandwich and moaned in her arms, we were
dying together; we never met again
although she was pregnant when I left her—I have
a daughter or son somewhere, darling grandchildren
in Norwich, Connecticut, or Canton, Ohio.
Every five years I think about her again
and plan on looking her up. The last time
I was sitting in New Brunswick, New Jersey,
and heard that her husband was teaching at Princeton,
if she was still married, or still alive, and tried
calling. I went that far. We lived
in Florence and Rome. We rowed in the bay of Naples

and floated, naked, on the boards. I started
to think of her again today. I still
am horrified by the cat's hunger. I still
am puzzled by the connection. This is another
insane devotion, there must be hundreds, although
it isn't just that, there is no pain, and the thought
is fleeting and sweet. I think it's my own dumb boyhood,
walking around with Slavic cheeks and burning
stupid eyes. I think I gave the cat
half of my sandwich to buy my life, I think
I broke it in half as a decent sacrifice.
It was this I bought, the red coleus,
the split rocking chair, the silk lampshade.
Happiness. I watched him with pleasure.
I bought memory. I could have lost it.
How crazy it sounds. His face twisted with cunning.
The wind blowing through his hair. His jaws working.

MAKING THE LIGHT COME

My pen was always brown or blue, with stripes
of gold or silver at the shaft for streaks
of thought and feeling. I always wore the nib
on the left side. I was a mirror right-hander,
not a crazy twisted left-handed cripple,
trying to live in this world, his wrist half broken,
his shoulder shot through with pain. I lived by smiling,
I turned my face to the light—a frog does that,
not only a bird—and changed my metal table
three or four times. I struggled for rights to the sun
not only because of the heat. I wanted to see
the shadows on the wall, the trees and vines,
and I wanted to see the white wisteria
hanging from the roof. To sit half under it.
Light was my information. I was an immigrant
Jew in Boston, I was a Vietnamese
in San Jose, taking a quick lunch hour,
reading Browning—how joyous—I was worshiping
light three dozen years ago, it led me
astray, I never saw it was a flower
and darkness was the seed; I never potted
the dirt and poured the nutriments, I never
waited week after week for the smallest gleam.
I sit in the sun forgiving myself; I know
exactly when to dig. What other poet
is on his knees in the frozen clay with a spade
and a silver fork, fighting the old maples,
scattering handfuls of gypsum and moss, still worshiping?

IT WAS A RISING

It was a rising that brought the worms. They came
when the bodies came, the air was muddy, it was
a small mistake, the fingers were gone, the lips
were eaten away—though I love worms, they have
bags on their backs and pointed sticks, they come
by the thousands, they can clean a beach in an hour,
they can clean the ground of fruit and bottles,
paper and plastic. I was a worm once, I wore
an olive uniform, my specialty was Luckies,
I speared them by threes, I hooked a bone to a cup,
I caught the silver foil. The rain when it comes
forces the worms to the surface; that is another
rising but not as cataclysmic. Love
of one thing for another brought them up,
and love will bring them back. This is the flesh
that dies and this is the flesh that lives. The bone
at the base of the spine is called the almond, it is
the nucleus of our birth. I had my chance
when the worms were in the air. I went out swimming,
I started to float, I held my arms up sideways
and let myself be eaten. I lie on the beach
planning my future. I am a mile away
from the motors out there and I am a yard away
from the wet footprints. There is a bird half crying
and there are the waves half moaning, these are the sounds.
My nose alone is showing, most of my head
is buried, I should have a straw in my mouth
to breathe with and a periscope for my eye
to see the flags and see the derrick. I lie
in coldness, only my lips are burning; I crack
my blanket, I am free again, I rise
with sand on my shoulder, stomach, thighs. The calcium
ruins my arm; I try to wipe my back
and scream in pain; I crash into the water;
it is my justice there, in the blue, in the brown,
and I am happy. I find my stone with one breath
and rub the hatchings. It is a rolled-up scroll.
It is a book. I swim a few short lengths,
to Ireland and back, and end up walking the planks.
It is either the dream of Asbury Park

where it is built on clouds and there are cherubs
holding it end on end, or it is the city
itself, a state senator at one end,
a Confederate Legionnaire at the other,
in front of Perkins, with an unlined notebook,
ready for my own visionary window,
ready for a whole morning of sunlight and silence.

HOBBES

I am here again
walking through the long-term parking,
fighting the cold.
My mind is on Hobbes,
how he would fare on the small bus,
what luggage he would carry,
what he would do with his meanness.
I climb the two steps
and with my two red eyes
I make peace with the driver.
He will drop me at Piedmont
and I will drag myself to another counter
and another nasty and brutish computer.
All is poor and selfish
sayeth the monster;
only pride and fear of death
move us.
I hold my little contract in my hand
and walk down the ramp all bloody and sovereign.
I give my number up
and lie down in my padded seat
and tie myself in.
After a while I will be warm and happy,
maybe when breakfast is being carried in,
maybe when lunch;
and though Hobbes be with me
I will sing in my seat
and fall asleep over Kansas and southern Utah.
I will wake in the dark
and put my left shoe on over one mountain
and my right shoe on over another.
When the time comes
I will put my ugly suitcase in the narrow aisle
and wait for the bodies in front of me.
He who meets me, or she,
will know me by my flower
or the lines around my eyes
or my wolf walk,
and I will be his or hers forever,

three full days or more.
I will live in the sunshine
and breathe the air
and walk up and down the brown grass
and the white cement.
I will keep the beast
in my breast pocket
or the inside of my briefcase
next to the wine stain and the torn satin.
Going back
I will reconsider all my odd connections
and prepare for that long slow descent
through Altoona and Harrisburg and Whitehouse, New Jersey,
by whispering and sighing as always.
If Hobbes is there
we will get on the Long Term bus together
and I will be his—or hers—forever,
two or three minutes or more,
at least until we reach the shelters.
I have my number in one of my twelve pockets
and he has his.
He sings, you know, in bed,
and still plays tennis,
not so bad for an Englischer.
We drift apart on Route 22
and Route 24, going west and east.
This was a lifetime friend,
although we'd be apart sometimes for years.
I know no one
who loved his own head more.
I'll tell this story:
when Charles II turned against him
he stayed in bed for seven days and nights
murdering bishops.
He wrote a complete version of the *Iliad* and the *Odyssey*
when he was ninety.
He never gave up his wild attempt
to square the circle.
I make the turn on Route 78
singing Villa-Lobos.
I am a second soprano.
Life has been good the past eight years,
the past two months.
I write a letter to myself

on force and fraud in the twentieth century.
I write a long and bitter poem
against the sovereign,
a bastard, whoremonger and true asshole,
as always, my darling.

GRAPEFRUIT

I'm eating breakfast even if it means standing
in front of the sink and tearing at the grapefruit,
even if I'm leaning over to keep the juices
away from my chest and stomach and even if a spider
is hanging from my ear and a wild flea
is crawling down my leg. My window is wavy
and dirty. There is a wavy tree outside
with pitiful leaves in front of the rusty fence
and there is a patch of useless rhubarb, the leaves
bent over, the stalks too large and bitter for eating,
and there is some lettuce and spinach too old for picking
beside the rhubarb. This is the way the saints
ate, only they dug for thistles, the feel
of thorns in the throat it was a blessing, my pity
it knows no bounds. There is a thin tomato plant
inside a rolled-up piece of wire, the worms
are already there, the birds are bored. In time
I'll stand beside the rolled-up fence with tears
of gratitude in my eyes. I'll hold a puny
pinched tomato in my open hand,
I'll hold it to my lips. Blessed art Thou,
King of tomatoes, King of grapefruit. The thistle
must have juices, there must be a trick. I hate
to say it but I'm thinking if there is a saint
in our time what will he be, and what will he eat?
I hated rhubarb, all that stringy sweetness—
a fake applesauce—I hated spinach,
always with egg and vinegar, I hated
oranges when they were quartered, that was the signal
for castor oil—aside from the peeled navel
I love the Florida cut in two. I bend
my head forward, my chin is in the air,
I hold my right hand off to the side, the pinkie
is waving; I am back again at the sink;
oh loneliness, I stand at the sink, my garden
is dry and blooming, I love my lettuce, I love
my cornflowers, the sun is doing it all,
the sun and a little dirt and a little water.
I lie on the ground out there, there is one yard
between the house and the tree; I am more calm there

looking back at this window, looking up
a little at the sky, a blue passageway
with smears of white—and grey—a bird crossing
from berm to berm, from ditch to ditch, another one,
a wild highway, a wild skyway, a flock
of little ones to make me feel gay, they fly
down the thruway, I move my eyes back and forth
to see them appear and disappear, I stretch
my neck, a kind of exercise. Ah sky,
my breakfast is over, my lunch is over, the wind
has stopped, it is the hour of deepest thought.
Now I brood, I grimace, how quickly the day goes,
how full it is of sunshine, and wind, how many
smells there are, how gorgeous is the distant
sound of dogs, and engines—Blessed art Thou,
Lord of the falling leaf, Lord of the rhubarb,
Lord of the roving cat, Lord of the cloud.
Blessed art Thou oh grapefruit King of the universe,
Blessed art Thou my sink, oh Blessed art Thou
Thou milkweed Queen of the sky, burster of seeds,
Who bringeth forth juice from the earth.

KNOWLEDGE FORWARDS AND
BACKWARDS

This was city living in the 1930s,
making machine guns out of old inner tubes,
fighting above the garages. It was peaceful
killing and spying and maiming; sometimes we smoked
cigars, or roasted potatoes—we used gloves
to reach into the coals; sometimes I put
a cinder to my lips, a charred and filthy
piece of wood, then stirred through the fire hunting
my lost potato. We were not yet assimilated,
nothing fit us, our shoes were rotten; it takes
time to adjust to our lives, ten and twelve years
was not enough for us to be comfortable—
after a while we learn how to talk, how to cry,
what causes pain, what causes terror. Ah, we had
stars, in spite of the sulphur, and there was dreaming
as we came into the forties. I remember
the movies we went to—I am spending my life
accounting now, I am a lawyer, the one
with blood on his lips and cash in his pockets. I reach
across for the piece of paper, it is cardboard
from one blue shirt or another, there are columns,
I whistle as I study them. There is
a seal on the boardwalk, just about the size
of a tiny burro, the one I rode was blind
and circled left, the miniature golf is the same,
the daisies are there on the seventh hole, the palms
are crooked as always, the fences are rusted, the windmills
are painted blue and white, as always, the ocean
is cold, I hated the ocean, Poseidon bounced me
over and over, I was gasping then,
trying to get a breath, and I am gasping
now, my rib is broken, or bruised, the muscle
inside the bone, or over the bone. I have
a hundred things to think about, my mind
goes back, it is a kind of purse, nothing
is ever lost. I wait for the pain to change
to pleasure, after a while my lips will stop moving,
I will stop moaning, I will start sleeping, one day
there is an end, even if at this end

there is lucidity and gruesome recollection
and I am paying for every red mark and blue mark.
I have the calendar in front of me;
I have the pencil at my lips, but no one
can live in place of us, there is no beast
on the seventh hole to save us; the grass is false,
it is a kind of cellophane, it is
produced in shops, above garages, maybe
in spare bedrooms or out of car trunks; there is
no spirit with her finger on her forehead
and her mouth open; there is no voice for sobbing
so we can sob with it a little, although—
and I am only beginning to feel this—I am
accumulating—what could I call it, a shadow?—
I am becoming a kind of demon, you turn
into a demon, with knowledge forwards and backwards,
backwards, forwards, you develop a power,
you develop a look, you go for months
with sight, with cunning, I see it in older men,
older women, a few of them, you stand
at some great place, in front of the Port Authority
or facing the ocean, you see the decade in front of you,
you see yourself out there, you are a swimmer
in an old wool suit, you are an angry cabbie,
you are a jeweler, you are a whore, the smell
of burned pretzels is everywhere, you walk
backwards and forwards, there is a point where the knot
is tied, you touch your fingers, you make a cage,
you make a roof, a steeple, at last you walk
forwards and backwards, your shirt is thin, your elbows
are getting longer, you are a type of demon,
you can go forth and forth, now it's the ocean
now it's the Port Authority, now you are sixty,
standing behind the pretzel man, amazed
at the noise around you, amazed at the clothes, amazed
at the faces; now you are twelve, you stand in a little
valley of water, you study the sand, you study
the sky, it was a violent journey, you end up
forgetting yourself, you stand at some place, there are
thousands of places, you stand in the Chrysler Building
beside the elevators, you stand in a lookout
on Route 78, you stand in the wooden post office
in Ocean Grove, in front of the metal boxes;
it is a disgrace to dance there, it is shameful
snapping your fingers, if we could just be singers

we'd walk down Main Street singing, no one as yet
has done this, three and four abreast, the language
could be Armenian, it could be Mohawk—
that is a dream too, something different from Whitman
and something different from Pound. What a paradise,
in front of the Quaker Inn, the women are watching,
I'm singing tenor, someone is taking a picture.
For me, when there is no hierarchy, for me,
when there is no degradation, when the dream
when lying is the same as the dream when walking,
when nothing is lost, when I can go forth and forth,
when the chain does not break off, that is paradise.

TWO MOONS

I'm looking at the moon, I'm half resting
on my right knee until the water settles.
There is a tree in the upper left-hand corner,
there is a house beside it. No one is watching,
I'm dying out here in the cold, I move my leg,
my knee is muddy, I shift to the other knee,
there are some waves between the cracks, there is
some grass inside the windows, it is marsh grass,
the blades are thick and sharp; I lean half over
to see my face, it is that Jewish face,
or Slavic face, that Spanish, I am grieved
by the lines around the eyes and by the fat
around the neck, around the chin; I stir
the water a little, near the mouth, a light
is coming on somewhere, someone is watching
me having my heart attack or dropping my key;
the moon is in its final phase, it drips
thick milk, there is a branch that looks like a calf,
it suckles the moon, it digs its feet in the ground,
its eyes are wild, the slaver is on its chin;
I have been still enough, I stand on my feet,
I stamp a little, the light goes out, I howl
silently, silently, I have learned that from dogs,
though I have learned when not to howl, I learned that
from parents and teachers, clerks and principals,
dentists and rabbis, doctors and lawyers—I hear
baying in Chile and baying in Africa,
men look up and see the moon, they scream
from pain, their backs are smashed, their faces are swollen,
their eardrums are broken, their genitals are purple,
there are welts from their shoulders to their buttocks,
they have been drinking gasoline, it is
too brilliant to bear, it should be dark, such beauty
is agonizing. There is a telephone wire
above the house, and a cigarette butt on the chimney
beside the grass, wet and useless. I drop
a stone in for a hurricane, there was
too much of crystal, I will leave when the sirens
go off, there will be a truck or an ambulance,
I will play footsie with the girl beside me,

she is nine, ah those are the girls that know me,
and love me and understand me, their poor mothers
are nervous, helpless. I am thinking of Yeats,
and Keats and Pound, on beauty. Somewhere a general,
somewhere a tall policeman is looking at the moon,
he wipes away some blood from his boot, there is
a tooth, and a piece of tongue, caught in the laces,
he waits for his daughter, she is nine, he gives her
a gentle touch, how gentle he is. Somewhere
up there the dust is falling, I have read it,
somewhere valleys and mountains, somewhere lake beds—
Darling Li Po, I bend my lips to the moon,
I wait for the tide, I touch myself with mud,
the forehead first, the armpits, behind the knees,
clothes or no clothes; now I walk on my face,
I had to do that, now I walk on the wires,
now I am on the moon, I am standing
between two moons, always there are two moons,
one for us and one for them, we know it,
visiting famous hills, following shadows,
believing in water, bowing to sparrows, bowing
to white deer, refusing to shame the spirit.

LYRIC

I wonder who has pissed here
and stared—like me—at those wild petunias
or touched a purple leaf from that small pear tree.

Has anyone lain down here
beside those red peppers
or under those weak elm withers
standing in shame there?

Dear God of that grape,
has anyone snapped off a little curlicue
to see if it's wood or wire
or stripped the bark off those thick vines
and leaned against that broken fence?

Has anyone put some old parsley in his mouth
to see what the taste is
or lifted a rose mum to his face
to see if he'll live forever?

MY FAVORITE FAREWELL

There is a kind of mop hanging down from the tree.
It is a willow. It has its own sad branches
somewhere. There is a huge Greek crypt
in front of the tree and there are stairs going down
to some kind of darkness. In the other corner
there are three cypresses—they stand alone
against a light blue sky—and there are flowers
around the crypt and bushes on the hillside.

Sadness is everywhere. Hector is holding
his wife's thin wrist and staring into her eyes.
Her hand is hanging loosely on his neck
and she is holding back her tears. A plume
is sitting on his helmet and a beard
is hanging from his neck; his skirt is made
of gorgeous pelts and there are purple thongs
around his leg tied in a little ribbon.

What else? The nurse is holding the baby. He is
enormous. Andromache's robes are flowing.
There are pompoms on her shoes and disks
holding her sleeves up, and her girdle. Her hair
is wavy and hanging to her waist but the nurse's
is just below her fluted ear. Hector
is resting his right hand on a shield—it's more
like a lopsided wheel. He doesn't have a spear.

What else? There is a pond underneath the cypresses
and they are on a hill. There is an effort
at vegetation beside the pond. Hector's
sleeves are rolled up. Andromache is in motion.
The crypt is out of proportion; the background is missing
on the left side; the steps seem to go up
instead of down; there is a violet filagree
behind the steps; the pillars are covered with disks.

It is my favorite farewell. As I watch it
I know Achilles will tear his helmet off
and drag his body through the dust, and I know
his enemies will spit on him and stab

him and the dogs will feed on his blood. I pay
attention to these things. It is the only
life we have. I am happy to be here
in front of the silk work and embroidery

watching them say goodbye. They will have to
make do with their sentiments and banalities.
That is all they have. Their hands are clumsy.
Their hills are unconvincing. Their clouds are muddy.
They are lucky to have the cypresses
and they are lucky that there's a streak of blue
behind the willow. I press against the glass.
There is a nail stuck inside the silk

that adds another oddness to the painting,
that makes it flat and distant and ruins illusion—
if there was any illusion—although it may
have fallen from the backing and slid down
the sky and down the shield and through the ribbons
into the dirt. I kiss the baby goodbye.
I kiss the nurse goodbye. The snow is falling
and I will be walking in the street half buried

inside my overcoat. I remember
the ending now. They put his white bones
in a golden box and wrapped it in soft purple
before they covered it up with dirt and stones.
That was a nice farewell—Andromache sobbing,
Hecuba howling, Helen tearing her hair out.
I think it is the cypresses that moved me
the most although it is the mop-faced willow

that is the center of the grief. The cypresses
are like a chorus standing on top of the sky
and moaning—they are moaning about the wind
and moaning about the narrow steps; they sit
on the edge of a hill, they hardly are planted, they whisper
about Achilles: "Think of Achilles," they whisper.
"Think of his tapered spear, think of his shield
with three kinds of metal, thicker than a wrist,

heavier than a door, think of lifting it
and holding it up with one huge hand while the other
searches the air and dances"—I find it moving

in spite of the stiffness and pallor of the figures,
in spite of the missing leg and floating branches.
It is my fondness for those souls. It is
my love of childish trees and light blue skies
and flowing robes. I have to be forgiven.

FOR ONCE

It was in southern Florida I reached
my foot across to trap a soul. He strayed
from one orange tile to another; he would live
for twenty seconds under my shoe, then run
to his door and pant an hour or two. I watched him
climb his wall. He turned his head and stared.
He lifted one gluey leg, then another.

He was from Enoch, one of the little false ones
full of mathematics and wizardry,
a slave to the moon. We yodeled and sang together—
it was like scraping chalk—I touched his throat.
It was translucent. I could see the spiders
going down his gullet. "Just one more song," I sang,
and there, two blocks from the ocean, six thousand years
into our era, we stood on the street and shouted.

There was a sunset somewhere. Someone cranked
a window open, as if to listen. Beyond that
there were our noises, an airplane droning, a car
beginning a trip, a baby screaming, a woman
yelling in Spanish. We stood beside each other—
if you could call that standing, and speculated.
We were mediators. I rubbed his head
and his yellow eyes began to close. The two of us
were getting ready for something—I could tell that—
before we lost each other.
                          I was left
with the bougainvillaeas and the narrow sidewalk
and the chain-link fences and the creeping vines.
I kept the music secret, walking south
on the left side of the road, beside the mosses.
Our sound was southern, mixed a little with Spanish,
mixed a little with French, and Creole. For once
there was no Polish, or German. I was adjusting
to the dunes and swamps, although there was some forties,
and thirties too; the last thing I did was whistle
and ring the fences. I was alone now and wandered
up and down those streets. I thought of the tail;
I thought of the heart. I don't know about the heart,

how many chambers there are, how cold it gets,
where it shunts the blood to, what the pulse is,
if it's a *clumsy* heart, if it can love
like ours can, if it can be grown again, if food
destroys it and exercise renews it, if memory
can make it flutter, if passion can make it flow.

This I thought about going south on one street
and east on another, picking up coconuts
and holding them to my ear, tearing the fronds up
and wearing them like a shawl. It was a kind
of happiness, shrieking and hollering in the tropics,
watching my skin grow dry and my blood grow thin,
wandering through a forest of cypress roots,
finding someone that old and wise. I loved it.

STEPS

There are two hundred steps between my house
and the first café. It is like climbing a ladder.
I gasp and pant as if I were pulling a mule,
as if I were carrying a load of dirt. I do
the journey twice—I left the key in the car
the first time down. There is another hill
above the first—the road to the car—another
one hundred steps. But I was born in Pittsburgh
and I know hills; I know that second rise
after a leveling off; I know the gentleness
between the two pair of steps, I know the wear
at the center, if it is stone, the soft splinters,
if it is wood, and I know the broken spaces,
the rhythm stoppers—railroad ties—but even
worse, I know the broken heights, four inches
and then a foot, and then another foot,
or fourteen inches, and the curves that carry you
around and around. There is a street on the South Side—
Pittsburgh again—that goes up hundreds of feet.
It is a stairs. I walked until my thighs
had turned to stone; and there were walkways like that
on the side of streets and cars that only made it
partway up, some turned around, some facing
the houses, abandoned cars. I am in Samos,
a village called Stavrinidhes, halfway up
the mountain of Ampelos. The town of Ampelos
is two miles away, a forty-minute walk.
I sit all day and watch. The sea is on my left.
The hills are all around me. Today is the walk
to Manolates, an hour and a half by foot,
a little less by car; it is a mulepath
up and down the ridges. I like the streets
in Ampelos. You climb for fifteen minutes,
your legs go slower and slower; this time there is
the long slope, the slant between the steps,
no relief at all, and there are two steps
twenty-five inches apiece, and there is a stairs
with a tree at the top, it is a kind of pyramid,
a kind of throne, the tree is a king, it sits there
painted white, and there is a waterfall

of steps, it almost pours. I touch a window
on my left, I touch a curtain, there is a trumpet vine
in front of the house, there is wisteria—
a limb that stretches half a block—I touch
a cactus, I touch a telephone pole, I reach
the hill above the town. The thing about climbing
is how you give up. I sit on a rock. I am
in front of a mountain. There's a white horse behind me,
there's a two-foot cypress beside me, it's already
burdened with balls. I am waiting for Hera,
she was born on this island. Zeus must have roared
on every mountain, he must have lifted a pine tree
to make a bed for them, or scooped out a valley.
Ah, Lord, she was too full of anger. The clock
says something on one side, something else on the other.
It rises above the houses. There are some towns
in Pennsylvania like this, and West Virginia;
I have sat on mountains. Imagine Zeus
in West Virginia, imagine the temple to Hera
in Vandergrift, P.A. My heart is resting,
my back feels good, my breathing is easy. I think
of all my apartments, all that climbing; I reach
for a goldenrod, I reach for a poppy, the cross
is German more than Greek, our poppies are pale
compared to these. I gave up on twenty landings,
I gave up in Paris once, it was impossible,
you reach a certain point, it is precise,
you can't go further; sometimes it's shameful, you're in
the middle of a pair of stairs, you bow
your head, your hand is on the rail; your breath
is hardly coming; sometimes you run to the top
so you can stop at the turning, then your legs burn,
sometimes they shake, while you are leaning over
and staring down the well or holding your arm
against the wall. Sometimes the stairs are curved,
that makes a difference, sometimes the risers are high,
sometimes there are too many turns, your knees
cannot adjust in time. Sometimes it's straight up,
landing after landing. Like a pyramid.
You have to lean into the steps, you have to
kneel a little to stop from falling backwards.
I turn around to look at the mountain. There is
a little path going up, some dirt and stones;
it would take two more hours. The wind is almost
roaring here—a gentle roar—the ocean

is green at first, then purple. I can see Turkey.
Who knows that I have given up? I hear
two women talking, I hear a rooster, there is
the back of a chimney, seventy bricks, there is
a cherry tree in blossom, there is a privy,
three hundred bricks to a side, there is a cat
moaning in Greek. You would look at the cherry tree,
you would rest your feet on a piece of marble,
you would be in semi-darkness; there are
dark pink cherries on the roof, the bowl
is sitting on a massive base, the floor
is dirt, there is no door. I wave to a donkey,
I read his lips, his teeth are like mine, I walk
to the left to see the oven, I count the bricks,
I look at the clock again, I chew my flower.

Index of Titles

Index of First Lines